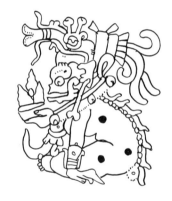

Editor: GARY GROTH
Associate Editor: MICHAEL CATRON
Designer: TONY ONG
Associate Publisher: ERIC REYNOLDS
Publishers: GARY GROTH and KIM THOMPSON

Fantagraphics Books, Inc.
7563 Lake City Way NE
Seattle, WA 98115

To receive a free catalogue of more books like this, as well as a wide variety of graphic novels, classic comic book and newspaper strip reprints, prose novels, art books, and cultural criticism, call 1 (800) 657-1100 or visit Fantagraphics.com.

Follow us on Twitter at @fantagraphics and on Facebook at facebook.com/fantagraphics.

Distributed in the U.S. by W.W. Norton and Company, Inc. (800) 233-4830

Distributed in Canada by Canadian Manda Group (800) 452-6642 x862

Distributed in the U.K. by Turnaround Distribution (44 020 8829-3002)

Distributed to comic book stores by Diamond Comics Distributors (800) 452-6642 x215

ISBN 978-1-60699-561-7

First Printing: August, 2012
Printed in Singapore

Published simultaneously:
The Lost Art of Ah Pook is Here
by Malcolm Mc Neill, Fantagraphics 2012

FANTAGRAPHICS BOOKS

MALCOLM MC NEILL

OBSERVED
WHILE
FALLING

Bill Burroughs, Ah Pook, and Me

For Orien

What follows is not a book about William Burroughs, neither is it a book about *Ah Pook*. It's certainly not a book about Me. It's an account of a blurring of those distinctions, of the line that supposedly separates and distinguishes them. With respect to the title, it's about the space *between* the names.

Bill Burroughs and I collaborated on a word/image novel for more than seven years. From a conventional perspective, the kind of interaction that inevitably involves a merging of ideas, a blurring of ownership. But Bill was not a conventional writer and Ah Pook is no ordinary character. In the course of the project there were occasions when the line between *fact* and *fiction, past* and *future* also dissolved.

Ah Pook is the Mayan death god. He implies a separation between the most significant of terms. A distinction considered absolute and unbreachable.

This book was written after that was shown not to be so.

"... *art makes us aware of what we know and what we don't know that we know*"

—WSB

LOS ANGELES

Dead Fingers Talk was the first thing that came to mind — a correspondence with a dead man.

When I began working with Bill, I'd found half-a-dozen pictures in a book that would become the inspiration for *Ah Pook is Here*. There was no description of the artist himself, just his images. Now, more than 30 years later, they'd resurfaced in another book and the artist had finally revealed himself. Not through pictures this time, but words.

It was a biography.

A textbook.

These were *facts*.

The artist was English, like me and, like me, he'd gone to art school in London. Like me, he'd met an American writer who happened to be living in London at the time. The writer had contacted *him* on the basis of *his* work, and they *too* had agreed to collaborate on a book together...

...about the Maya.

They'd met in Leicester Square, a few hundred yards down the street from where I'd met Bill. The artist had then moved to America to complete the work — just as I had — slightly ahead of his partner.

In Manhattan, his first home, like mine, was on Houston Street. He *also* had a studio in Tribeca.

From there we both moved to Prince Street.

We each had children born in New York, and each of us was separated from our wives there. His son, also born in December, was 6 years old at the time, as was mine.

We both quit illustration there.

As artists we shared a particular image style. In New York we'd become known for it — he through the panoramic images he exhibited in his gallery while living on Prince Street, myself through the panoramic images I created for television, while *also* living on Prince Street.

My images had led to a career as director. They were the reason I was now in California.

He also moved to California and while there, like me, became an American citizen — he while living in Solano *County*, me while living in Solano *Canyon*.

Facts.

Ultimately he produced a folio edition of his collaboration, describing the history of the project and acknowledging the friendship that had occurred as a result.

His account had already been published...

A hundred and fifty-nine years ago.

Now that I was aware of this, my own account could begin.

"The Mayan codices are undoubtedly books of the dead; that is to say, directions for time travel. If you see reincarnation as a fact, then the question arises: how does one orient oneself with regard to future lives?"

— AH POOK IS HERE

BILL BURROUGHS 1

LONDON
1970

Hornsey College of Art was supposedly one of the three best art schools in England. The prospectus showed a classic Victorian building surrounded by trees, situated in London's Crouch End. Apart from figure drawing classes, Friday Night Film shows, and the infamous Sit-in, however, I would spend very little time there. The Main College was still home to a couple of departments, but the rest were spread out in an eclectic assortment of buildings across North London.

The Graphics Department — where I *did* three years — was a former army barracks alongside the North Circular Road. Bowes Road, as it was called, was a very old barracks. A one-time recruitment center for the Middlesex Volunteers, it looked like a barracks and it felt like a barracks. Everything about it was contrary to what I thought an art school would be.

The Fine Art Department on the other hand, was located in the Alexandra Palace. A spectacular building with a glass-domed Palm Court, built in 1873, on a hill overlooking seven acres of parkland and most of London beyond. *Ally Pally*, as it was called[1], was where I really wanted to be.

My application to study Fine Art was turned down in favor of Graphics. In those days, English kids were paid to go to art school. Their tuition fees were covered and they were given a living allowance, none of which needed to be repaid. Colleges, in turn, received funding based on the number of students they graduated.

As a result, I was advised to become an Illustrator — a future, I was assured, that would benefit us both. A commercial artist that is, not a fine one. It was an arrangement I wasn't happy with. Fine artists were supreme in the hierarchy of image-makers. Illustrators were beneath them. They made art in a palace. We made do with a barracks.

It was a dismal place. Three years worth of students crammed into pokey little rooms, with pokey little windows and ceilings you could almost touch. Stables converted into darkrooms on one side, and the North Circular Road with its traffic on the other. If you were lucky enough to get a window seat you could see it. If not, you just heard it. Every day, nine to five.

For my flatmate Eddie and I, it was three years of long rush hour commutes, lugging portfolios back and forth from one double-decker bus to another. Showing up at nine a.m., sometimes soaked to the skin, in order to stare at a wall and try to be inspired. Try to come up with a more efficient design for the dialing instructions inside public payphones say, or a logo for an imaginary pub.

I hated type. In those days you had to painstakingly trace every letter out of giant typeface books to get the arrangement you 'needed,' then go downstairs to the compositing room and painstakingly assemble it backwards with wood and metal blocks. Then wait for it to get it printed. A procedure carried out by two ancient gentlemen in brown lab coats who'd conceivably been there longer than the building. Fortunately, a breakthrough occurred around that time: press type. Now you could painstakingly scrub letters directly down onto the paper — one after the other with a ballpoint pen. When it came to type, I sometimes hid out in the men's room for entire classes.

The only practical lasting instruction I recall was in photography. Vincenzo Ragazzini had been head of the Experimental Photography School in Rome and for some unaccountable reason had enlisted at Bowes Road. He taught darkroom tricks which I later applied to illustration. Apart from that, it was a group of well-intentioned, encouraging folks who actually demonstrated very little.

In order to graduate I had to write two papers: one on an artist of choice, the other on an art-related subject. I chose "Egon Schiele" — to me, the ultimate draftsman — and "Visual Narrative," a history of the process of using images to tell story; from the Egyptians, Greeks, Romans and Maya up to the present day Sunday Funnies." Having done that, I was good to go.

I was discharged in the spring of 1970.

I'd been working on sequential imagery ideas on my own in the meantime, trying to figure out a way of making self-contained narrative episodes in the form of freestanding paintings. I thought that if I could put a magazine together which featured that kind of work, as well as conventional comics and other forms of word/image narrative, I'd have the financial means for continuing with the idea. It would be an English version of the kind of magazines that were being produced in California by

R. Crumb, S. Clay Wilson, etc. During the final term at Bowes Road, I'd found several artists around London who were up for it.

A friend mentioned the idea to Graham Keen, graphics editor of *International Times* magazine, a London underground newspaper, who was interested in the same kind of idea. We should pool our resources, he said.

After an unsuccessful group attempt at deciding on a name, Keen phoned a couple of days later to inform me it was *Cyclops* — did I want to do the cover and advertiser's rate card? He had this much to spend, etc. Also he'd convinced a writer friend to contribute. When he'd shown him the artwork of the available artists, the writer had pointed at mine and said, *"I'll work with this guy."* It was a great opportunity, said Keen. I'll send you the text as soon as I get it.

In no time it wasn't *our* magazine anymore — and it wasn't an *English* one either. Keen's 'backer,' Matt Hoffman, was American and so was his writer friend.

Some guy named William Burroughs.

It wasn't so remarkable that I didn't know anything about him. In London — in 1970 — he was far from the celebrity he would later become. I read a lot, but he just wasn't an author I'd been drawn to.

When Keen announced Burroughs wanted to work with me, I was fairly indifferent. I was far more concerned with the way the magazine was headed. After his phone call, my enthusiasm for the entire project went downhill.[2]

Thinking it was only a matter of time before I quit, I didn't research Burroughs at all. In talking about the idea with friends though, I did discover a couple of things about him: he was American, a political writer, a junky, and he'd shot and killed his wife — despite which, somehow he was gay. A bio that didn't really resonate with my English art-kid way of life so far. I hadn't so much as smoked a joint, had never fired a gun, and I certainly wasn't gay.

As far as politics were concerned, in the spring of 1968, Hornsey art students had been the first to take over and close down their college. Ostensibly in protest over restrictions to making art, it rapidly became a forum for just about anyone with a political agenda. Marxists, Anarchists, Trade Union activists, anti-Vietnam War activists, among others, capitalized on a well publicized event to air their beefs. One speaker, Tariq Ali, harangued the students for not being political *enough*:

"You're artists!" he shouted. *"Do something!"*

"Like what?" we shouted back.

"Paint the walls!" he said.

Everyone laughed.

The muddle of art theory and left wing agendas[3] that followed short-circuited whatever political sense I might have had. It was my first exposure to the 'revolutionary' mindset. When the rhetoric went from practical restraints to making art, to the obligations of art to society, to the restructuring of society altogether, it was difficult to know what was what anymore. *"Smash the System"* and *"Don't Let the Bastards Grind You Down"* became the slogans for the event, but what did they have to do with Van Gogh or Leonardo Da Vinci?

The Vietnam War may have been bad, but that was America's problem. The pictures of My Lai would be published the following year, and the year after that, those of Kent State. The U.S. was a mess, but since I didn't live there, and wasn't threatened with the draft, what did it have to do with me? Like most English people I knew, my sense of America came from television, movies, and newspapers. Typically it wasn't very flattering. Right around the time of the Sit-in, we learned that Martin Luther King and Robert Kennedy had both been murdered. Who in their right mind would *want* to live there?

When Keen handed me the first batch of Burroughs's text, this overall disparity became painfully obvious. I'd thought that if I could come to terms with Beckett and Joyce, I shouldn't have a problem with anyone. Mr. Burroughs, though, was beyond me. And as far as 'comic strip' was concerned, gave me very little to work with. No real scenes, no character descriptions, no dialogue. Just a first person consideration of something called "Control" alternating between references to people and things I'd never heard of. It was called *The Unspeakable Mr. Hart* and it read like a text book. The first sentence set the tone:

"Mr. L. Ron Hubbard has postulated a Reactive Mind designed and implemented to inhibit creation or destruction and keep things on a sound financial basis... Other investigators such as Freud have also postulated such self defeating mechanisms but considered these as integral parts of the human psyche

rather than parasitic implants quite deliberately imposed by interested parties."

And so on. A total of 600 words in all, that I somehow had to illustrate and fit onto a single page.

The only thing to do was find phrases or ideas that I could visualize such as *"industrial giants"* ... *"Mayans"* ... *"something between a tape recorder and a virus,"* etc., and arrange them in frames like a comic strip. Then run the type as a block down the side.

... The Unspeakable Mr. Hart ... dinosaurs, electronic gadgets, Mayans...

It was an inauspicious start, and the result was far from impressive. I wasn't looking forward to the next installment.

Cyclops was a large format newspaper — 11 inches by 17 inches — similar to other underground publications such as *International Times* and *Friends*. *Cyclops* No. 1 appeared in July 1970. Along with *Mr. Hart*, I produced three other pages of my own and an image for the cover. In keeping with the American trend, the first issue also featured a strip by Vaughn Bodé, one of several American artists the paper promised to include in the future.

The next batch of text turned out to be easier. There were scenes, dialogue, and action. Mr. Hart himself was introduced, including his childhood and days at Harvard. There were Egyptian and Mayan images and even a murder. There were also a lot fewer words and enough visual material to expand it into a double-page spread.

... Mr. Hart, Clinch Smith, Harvard, Egyptian art, Mayan art ...

Episode 3 reverted back to the alternating 'textbook,' factual-fictional narrative style. Even so, it had a Mayan scene and opened a lot more image possibilities. The amount of reference material required meant it also took a lot longer to put together, so I decided to drop my other pages.

... cops, cadavers, executions, newspapers ...

I asked Keen if I could talk to Mr. Burroughs to get a sense of what was going on and where the story was headed, but for some reason it didn't happen. It was a surreal arrangement.

I decided to try and get a clue from other things he'd written and borrowed a copy of *Naked Lunch*. It didn't help.

Episode 4 continued the same way. The action still revolved around Hart, but the first person considerations continued to suggest more specific imagery. Whatever it was, I felt like I was getting better at it.

... cops, cadavers, executions, Mayan ceremonies ...

On the downside, as a replacement for my original cover strip, the first three pages featured a reprint of the American newspaper series *Flash Gordon*, a 'straight' comic from the 1930s. With that, the idea of an alternative English magazine disappeared altogether, and inevitably, since the paper clearly had no sense of direction, *Cyclops* No. 4 turned out to be the last.

I wasn't expecting to hear from Keen again, but very soon after, he phoned me. *"You'll be getting a call this afternoon,"* he said, *"you might want to be there."*

Around three o'clock, for the first time, I heard the remarkable voice of the man himself: Mr. William S. Burroughs.

"I want to meet the guy who knows how to draw me!" he intoned and insisted we meet.

Considering I'd really had no idea what I'd been doing for four months, it was an odd proposition.

Number 8, Duke Street, was a couple of blocks south of Piccadilly Circus; a narrow, nondescript building with a small, rickety elevator.

It opened directly into flat number 22, where Mr. Burroughs was waiting to greet me. He introduced himself as Bill.

The first thing that struck me was that he was wearing a jacket and tie — around the house — and not, I imagined, for my benefit. He was older than I'd expected, soft spoken, and polite.

The short hallway opened into the living room and small kitchen area. The furniture was unremarkable. Functional. No curves. More like an office, I thought. There were small desert watercolors on the walls. Kind of '50s looking. *"... by Mr. Brion Gysin,"* I was informed — who shared the flat.

The place was completely silent.

It was the middle of the afternoon and Mr. Burroughs was eating bacon. He invited me to join him. We sat on either side of a long polished table, with a few strips each, eating with our fingers. The end of one of his, I noticed, was missing.

When we were done, he lit up the first of many Senior Service cigarettes and brought up the subject of the visit.

"So," he said. *"You're the guy who knows how to draw me. How d'ya do that?"*

I hadn't intended to make Mr. Hart look like Burroughs. Even if I had known what he looked like, it would hardly have made sense to draw him as the villain. As a younger version of himself, however, the likeness *was* remarkable. An "identikit" picture he called it.

"I've no idea," I said.

He asked if anything like that had ever happened before. I told him that when I was younger, I used to draw pictures of a boy who appeared at the dinner table sometimes.

"Who was he?"

"I don't know. I was the only one who ever saw him."

"Did he ever call?"

"No."

He then asked how old I was.

I was 22 when I started working on *Cyclops*. Earlier that month I'd turned 23. He found this amusing. *"It's an auspicious number,"* he said, but didn't explain why.

We talked about *Cyclops*. How it had started. Why it had folded. The difficulties I'd had with the text. Now that it was over, I asked if he'd mind telling me what happened next. How did it end up? What was it about?

He was more than happy to oblige.

During the next couple of hours, he introduced me to the Reactive Mind, the Mayan Codices, Bishop Landa, Control, Cut-ups, the Word as Virus, The Algebra of Need, Randolph Hearst, and whole lot of other things that it 'was about.' How it ended up, though, he couldn't say. He hadn't written much beyond what I'd already seen.

The reason for the meeting had been simply to acknowledge an odd coincidence. Now that *Cyclops* was over, the idea of continuing with Mr. Hart hadn't been a consideration. By the end of the afternoon, though, we were talking about ways we might be able to do just that. A book maybe, a full-length novel. Not a comic book, but a *visual narrative* where pictures and text interacted in whatever form seemed appropriate. We agreed to meet again to talk further.

It was dark when I left. When I stepped out of the elevator, I felt like I was in a completely different world.

Things were never the same again.

In the second meeting, he gave me 11 pages of text:

The beginning was a countdown 23 seconds before 'Little Boy,' destroyed Hiroshima. A Japanese couple have sex and two small boys masturbate to coincide with the explosion. Counting down from 23 is an *"old sex game,"* apparently.

Hart's childhood and time at Harvard remained the same, but a scene with his drunken father trying to give him a sex talk had been added. Words that are wasted on young Hart, who feels neither pleasure nor pain.

It was great start but then it reverted back to methods again.

Having found the lost Mayan books, Hart is ready to set up his Control Machine. In his role as newspaper tycoon, his obsession with the images of fear and death continues, but now with a more extensive list of instructions regarding the kind of pictures his photographers must find and the ways in which his *artists* must enhance them. What he actually does with these pictures, however, was difficult to understand. The images he needed had to be so bad that he *couldn't* print them. Just a *"whiff"* was enough for what he had in mind. They are never actually shown, simply hinted at on *"computerized associational networks."*

"Mr. Hart intends to monopolize the pictures that others can't stand to see. Then he will never have to show them."

Having accumulated his store of "UGLY" words and pictures, Hart then uses the rage and fear contained within them against various people who get in the way of his research.

An example is "Percy Jones."

Jones is experimenting with speech scramblers — a means for *"getting inside"* people's heads, an idea Hart wants to corner for his own purposes. He hires 'the Whisperer' to take care of him, a character who has the knack of projecting his voice in such a way that other people appear to be doing the talking. He follows Jones, 'whispering' obscenities so that those around him become unaccountably abusive and threatening. Jones is reduced to a nervous wreck and his research comes to an end.

Hart then switches his attention to viruses — the perfect delivery system for infecting his victims with the images of their own death; images augmented by his *stable of artists* who combine them with the features of particular viruses.

Drawings are made of cold sores and people *with* cold sores in order to *"draw out the cold sore feeling."* Drawings of hepatitis and encephalitis are enhanced the same way so that Hart can *"draw the virus onto any body just as he drew a synthetic anti-Jones virus onto Jones."*

The virus of choice is rabies. Once the symptoms develop, no one survives it. By understanding the mechanisms involved, Hart is on the verge of creating viruses to order. Push button plagues with specific targets.

But *"then disaster strikes"* —

Scientists announce that any gene can now be created synthetically. Any country can now produce viruses for which there is no cure. To compound matters, a 6-year-old boy in Ohio survives rabies. He has survived death and become death for Mr. Hart.

"Little Boy" has come home to roost.

Hart dies.

As a kind of afterthought, the final page introduces 23-year-old Audrey Carsons, who experiences the effects of a rabid bat bite.

Compared to what he'd talked about at our first meeting, it was anti-climactic and, as far as a book was concerned, as difficult as it had been with *Cyclops.* Apart from Percy Jones and Hiroshima, there were no real scenes, just a long exposition of Hart's methods. Methods that now included many references to artists and drawing — an idea that was confusing for other reasons.

When I was working on *Cyclops,* I really knew nothing about Burroughs. Even so, I'd somehow made Mr. Hart look just like him. Mr. Hart the *bad* guy, that is.

Hart the newspaper tycoon, who was loosely based on Randolph Hearst, came from a wealthy background, went to Harvard to study the Mayans, then set out to discover the secrets of Control. In our first meeting, Burroughs revealed that he, too, came from a wealthy background and had also studied the Mayans at Harvard. He, too, was fascinated by the control system conceivably contained within their books.

Writers naturally create surrogates of themselves in their fiction but this seemed a bit extreme, especially since the character now *looked* like him. Burroughs's alter ego was also contemporary; the events that precipitate his downfall occur in 1970. The author was writing himself into his own book.

With all the references to artists and drawing, he now appeared to be writing *me* in as well. He'd even introduced a 23-year-old protagonist. The line between fact and fiction was somewhat fuzzy here. Who exactly was talking to who?

It was oddly disconcerting but then who was I to argue? In the book, or out of the book, my role was the same. Mr. Hart/Mr. Burroughs was quite clear on that — in caps no less:

"GO OUT AND GET THE PICTURES. THE UGLY PICTURES. IF YOU CAN'T FIND THEM MAKE THEM. AND IF YOU CAN'T MAKE UGLY PICTURES YOU'RE JUST NOT UGLY ENOUGH FOR THIS JOB."

Drawing a *"whiff"* of something that couldn't be shown seemed like a tricky proposition, so I decided to let it slide for a while; along with the *"computerized associational networks"* on which the *"whiffs"* were to be *"hinted"* at.

My first assignment, I decided, was to look for viruses.

The Gordon Museum, Guy's Hospital is the oldest and largest of its kind. Medical memorabilia have been accumulating there since the 1800s. Since it's only accessible to the 'trade,' a medical student friend sneaked me in as an 'Operating Theatre Technician.'

We were the only visitors. Along with the bones of giants, dwarves, and several-headed babies, we were treated to the preserved remains of murder victims, bizarre suicides, dissected criminals, abnormal births, and human anomalies of every description. Pickled organs and body parts in jars rounded out the show.

Anatomy was something I'd studied in Art school and I'd taught myself taxidermy as a teenager.[4] Guts and dead bodies didn't bother me. This was bodies from a different point of view, though: Mr. Hart's point of view. These images were to be recorded and manipulated in order to *create* fear and death. There was certainly evidence of it here.

The skull of a woman caved in with an axe; the stomach of a suicide who'd swallowed scalding water; the arm and shoulder of a man, flash-fried when it had touched the third rail. In terms of the assignment, there was also plenty of disease, but disease often leaves little of *itself* behind. Viruses are self-serving microscopic termites that burrow into flesh and bone until all that's left are the ravaged remains of the victim. Even those would disappear if not for formaldehyde and extremely competent sculptors.

A hanged man had been sliced into sections horizontally from head to foot then perfectly modeled in wax. (Even the rope tear on his neck had been faithfully reproduced.) Studying the slices close up was a disquieting sensation. Nothing in the intricate arrangement of tissues was extraneous or arbitrary. Everything worked toward a single purpose: to sustain life. All of which was beyond our comprehension or control.

Viewed on a larger scale, the human body had the mystery and complexity of an alien landscape. On a molecular level, unknown to the sum of its parts, it was accident and opportunity waiting to happen. Manipulating such forces would be a monumental undertaking, as Mr. Hart would discover. Drawing pictures to express that idea, likewise. What death *looked like* was apparently a secondary consideration. As Bill had indicated, it was about drawing out *"...the feeling."*

... virus patterns ... diseased faces ... cadavers ...

The same friend also gave me a couple of illustrated textbooks from the early 1900s dealing with viruses and skin diseases. I brought them with me on my next visit to Duke Street. I also found photo scrap for Hiroshima and Percy Jones, and, for Mayan reference, I brought a couple of books about pre-Colombian civilizations. To round out the pile, I threw in some 'tasteful' porno.

He examined the porno first. Raising his glasses to study the pictures more closely. Several of them featured two girls and a guy. He handed them back.

"No question about the star of the show," he said, referring to the guy's cock.

We talked about the similarities between the Mayans and the Egyptians and he suggested we visit the British Museum sometime to check them out. He asked to borrow the Mayan books, but he had nothing new to show me.

A couple of days later, he called to tell me he'd made an appointment at the British Museum to look at a copy of the Dresden Codex — one of the three Mayan books that had survived the book burnings of Bishop Landa in the 1560s.

The British Museum: seven million artifacts stretching back to the dawn of history. Millions upon millions of artists long gone. I'd been there many times.

It was raining that day. By the time I'd walked the half-mile from the Underground, I was soaked. Bill met me inside the entrance, his glasses, raincoat, and hat also soaked.

We were ushered into the reading room and a small blue cardboard box was placed reverentially on the table before us. In the scope of its surroundings, an unremarkable and seemingly insignificant object measuring 8½ inches long by 4 inches wide by 2½ inches deep. Inside were an explanatory booklet and a stack of hand-colored line drawings. Images, we were informed, that had been created from tracings made in 1932, from tracings made in 1826, of the actual Codex in Dresden.

The original is a piece of parchment 11 feet long, folded accordion style into 74 vertical pages. Both sides are illustrated, creating a single continuous image. The pages are divided into two, three, or four horizontal levels reminiscent of a miniature comic book; a word/image narrative comprised of cartoon-like characters and explanatory glyphs.

Closer inspection revealed it to be far from comic. There was nothing fanciful or arbitrary about the designs. Each line and shape clearly had a specific intent. These were *instructions* — information conveyed by the smartest mathematicians, astronomers, biologists, sociologists, and spiritual luminaries of their day. Given the remarkable accuracy of Mayan calendrics and astronomical computation, this was the product of extraordinary intelligence and sensibility.

Smart as they were, though, it seemed unlikely these mathematicians and scientists had done the drawings themselves. The eye-hand coordination and design sense necessary to make these pictures suggested individuals trained — or born to the purpose. These guys were good. As any designer could see, the quality of the line and the decisions made in the orchestration of the characters was the work of competent draftsmen — people who could draw; people who could draw out the ideas of others.

This was word/image collaboration at its best, working toward the ultimate goal: *to make it happen*. Much of the direction contained in these books referred to events yet to occur; planetary configurations that would determine social ritual and civic behavior in the years, decades, even centuries to come. Here was the system of Control unique to the Maya.

I wondered about the process of creating such books. These were government textbooks, after all. Was there a bureaucracy involved? A bevy of middlemen passing things along? Studio bosses, creative directors, art directors and designers — all handing it off to the guys who actually did the work? The 'wrists' as they're called. Lots of — *"I think what the boss really wants here is..."* etc. being passed down the line. These books were probably the result of centuries of such delegation.

But what about the original process — the moment when the ideas were first conceived? Surely that was a more intimate arrangement: a back and forth between word and image directly. A wise old man sitting at home, maybe — in a jacket and tie even — imparting his ideas, one-on-one to an eager young artist.

Like its Paris and Madrid counterparts, the Dresden Codex is partially destroyed. Much of its content has since been deciphered, but thanks to the good Bishop and his cronies, the essence of Mayan culture has been lost forever. The experience and intellectual strivings of millions of human beings accumulated over centuries, reduced to less than a handful of battered, incomplete books.[5]

The Dresden Codex has outwitted the flames twice. Having escaped the onslaughts of the Spaniards, it disappeared into obscurity and remained hidden for hundreds of years. Then it resurfaced in Germany, provenance unknown, and, two centuries later, escaped the appalling fire-bombing of Dresden in World War II. Twelve pages were damaged and several were lost in that conflagration, but most of the codex — and the ideas that compelled it — persevered.

It was a magical book.

For an hour or so, we looked at the pictures and made notes, punctuated by Bill's trips outside for a Senior. As we were leaving we ordered a photocopy — an enormous undertaking in those days, especially in

England where everything takes that much longer. A couple of weeks later, Bill called to say it had arrived.

We took turns studying the codex, creating character sheets together for the various gods, and figuring out color schemes to suit. We found the names in one of the books I'd loaned Bill.

I'd borrowed it from the Hornsey college library for my graduation paper on Visual Narrative, but since that was around the time *Mr. Hart* had appeared, I'd decided to keep on borrowing it. It was a perfect example of the way collaboration works and the devious way an idea reveals itself: On one of the pages, positioned one above the other, were images of Yum Pax — the young corn god, Ah Puch — the death god[6] and Ix Tab — the hanged goddess of ropes and snares — an arrangement that understandably appealed to Bill.

I also discovered Hunab Ku, the god of whom no image was made. As the invisible head of the Maya Control machine, he fit right in with the *"whiff"* of something only to be *"hinted at."*

... *Mayan codex images ... glyphs ... god sketches ...*

A few weeks later Bill suggested another get together. He'd figured out the gist of the story:

It's unlikely, he said, that only three Mayan books survived Bishop Landa's bonfire. Artifacts 'disappearing' during conflicts such as these have been a feature of culture since images and writing began. Books, manuscripts, maps, diagrams, and artworks have subsequently ended up in the private collections of the wealthy and powerful. A preemptive measure, as it were, for making sure that those in control stayed that way. Such artifacts, and the information contained within them, were then — and still are — inaccessible to the world at large. It's also possible that the Maya didn't cough up the entire library and there are more books waiting to be found.

Mr. Hart addressed both issues: He's a rich collector of any knowledge that can possibly further his aims of Control and, as a Mayan scholar, he's convinced that other books exist. Given that these books possibly reflect the controlling methods of the Mayan priesthood, he's anxious to get his hands on them. Having done that, however, he finds himself confronted with a worldview entirely alien to his either/or, good-versus-evil, Judeo/Christian ethic. Convinced that the secret of control lies in the manipulation of the images of fear and death, he unleashes a very different version of the idea into the world:

Ah Pook the Destroyer!

These are not ordinary books. They are manuals for time travel. Instructions for *manipulating* time. Mr. Hart, the Ugly American, has unwittingly taken on an adversary beyond his understanding and opened a Pandora's box of disease, destruction — and ultimate retribution.

The Mayan gods had been invoked. Mutant boy heroes were now also using the books, using Words and Images to access the future, locate Audrey Carsons and his friend Guy Smith, and bring down Hart's Control machine. Together, they will put an end to the controlling human condition forever.

It was a book about Death and traveling through time. A book called *Ah Pook is Here*.

I was a kid in a candy store.

... Cumhu the lizard boy, Ouab the cat, Xolotl the salamander
... color techniques ... rough scenes ...

There was no mention of money. I didn't have any and neither did Bill. My only means for continuing with the project was freelance illustration jobs, which, when you're just out of art school, are few and far between. And none of it pays much.

How to go about finding it, and the business of getting paid for it, were not part of the art school curriculum. The idea that I might go weeks without work, or work on a project and then wait months to get paid — or not get paid at all — had for some reason been omitted. Apparently, it could only be learned the hard way. It was par for the course. But alternating *Ah Pook* with such a precarious routine would be the norm for years to come.

... Mexican firing squad ... Los Alamos ... the moon ...

Lack of money was simply a feature of the overall unreality. I wasn't prepared for it, but I wasn't surprised by it, either. Neither were most of my friends.

To balance things out, at that age there are plenty of distractions. In the first couple of months of 1971, there were a few that changed things irrevocably.

First, my flatmate Alan bought *Led Zeppelin II*. He stuck headphones on me, cranked up "Whole Lotta Love," and said *"Smoke this."*

At five-and-a-half minutes, it was the perfect length for my first joint.

A few days after that, friend Bob stopped by and suggested I *"Swallow this."*

When it kicked in, we were in the National Portrait Gallery in Trafalgar Square. I'd been there many times, but this was the first time I'd realized how funny it was. Giottos, Mantegnas, even Botticellis were suddenly hilarious. Eyes weren't level, perspectives were off, heads were too big... and the colors were *insane*. The best exhibit of all turned out to be a fire extinguisher. Odder yet were the military-looking guards patrolling the place. When one of them warned us about laughing too much, we decided we'd better leave.

Outside St James's Palace, we were confronted by another military figure: a bright red one this time with an enormous fur hat, standing perfectly still in front of a kennel of some sort. We studied him for quite a while until two equally improbable characters strode onto the scene. *Sinister* characters, also in big hats. Coppers!

Heading toward Piccadilly, we discovered a bookshop. Propped in the window was a book titled *BOSCH*. My favorite painter. I bought it immediately. Further along was a movie theatre. On the marquee it said: THE DEVILS — DIRECTED BY KEN RUSSELL. We went straight in.

The next time I saw Bill I had a lot more to talk about.

Naturally, Timothy Leary came up. Leary, said Bill, was *"sloshing around in the metaphysical slop-bucket."* Personally, Bill didn't care for LSD... but would I care for some opium? It was a mellower smoke than grass, and he gave me some to take home. In trade, I loaned him the Bosch book.

... drug busts ... plane hijacking ... mutants ... Death Academy ... guns ...

Bill never directly advocated drugs of any kind, certainly not LSD. He'd had two bad trips, he said, and would never touch it again. *"...horrible stuff,"* he said. *"...I just don't want to know about acid."*[7]

As it happened, LSD ironically provided the inroad to his worldview. It clearly demonstrated the dichotomy of absurdity and terror that characterized his writing. My first experience with it was an indelible image of Control and the Reactive Mind at work.

The drug exposed the tenuous nature of agreed-upon reality. How the minutest quantity of chemical substance — something no bigger than the proverbial head of a pin — could change one's perception entirely. It confirmed in the most dramatic way, that *everything* was subject to question.

> *... future trip ... deserts ... snakes ... cities ... running crowds*
> *... orgone ray guns ...*

By the end of the year, the text included the FBI, hijacked airliners, Mexican bandits, Virus B23, burning cities, and an old Gombeen woman. Cumhu, the Lizard Boy had taken a trip into the future, killed his father, and stolen the secret Mayan books. Bosch's *Garden of Earthly Delights* became the set for the final scene. A character named Old Sarge had appeared to instruct the young protagonists in the ways of dying and organize them for Armageddon.

Old Sarge was one of Bill's recurring characters; the eternal no-nonsense army man, imparting the *"broad general view of things"* to the young recruits. Given the age disparity, I naturally identified with the younger characters: Cumhu, Audrey, Ouab, etc. On the other hand, I saw Bill in the likes of Old Sarge and the Dib — a half-dead/half-alive embodiment of Ah Pook. And of course, Mr. Hart.

> *... The Dib, Jimmy the Shrew ... lunar landscape ... trains ... flesh gardens ...*
> *diseased boys ... St Louis carnival ... Cumhu's father ...*

Looking for reference material in those days was an analog process. Sitting at home in your skivvies and just clicking a couple of times with a mouse was an option yet to come. The right picture of a Mexican bandit, say, or an atomic bomb, meant a trip to a library, a bookstore, or another illustrator. Sometimes days could go by without finding it. Multiplied by the amount of imagery that Bill was cooking up, it became an ongoing, frustrating, and sometimes impossible task. On the other hand, actually *going somewhere* to find stuff made the search itself an integral part of the process.

For airplane reference, naturally, I went to the airport. A ground crew friend drove me out onto the tarmac at Heathrow and we wandered around inside planes being cleaned after arrival. Nobody paid us any mind. A baggage handler even showed me how to 'pop open' a suitcase.

I found Mexican bandits at a Mexican Cultural Library. As with most book image reference, I read the books as well.

American cops, trains, and cities were obviously images I was aware of, but not in the specific way that the project required. I found image scrap for most of it but decided to try adapting English architecture as an easier alternative. It was the process of determining whether it would work or not that resulted in *Ah Pook's* first real encounter with Control.

In England at that time, the police were known ironically as the 'Old Bill.'

I was walking home late one night studying the tops of buildings, when I noticed a cop car moving slowly alongside me on the far side of the street. The moment I saw him, the driver slammed on the brakes and shouted " *Up against the wall!*" A bit dramatic, I thought, especially coming from inside a Morris Minor[8], but I wasn't going to argue. I did as I was told and he and his partner clattered across the street with their 'torches' to search me.

Explaining that I wasn't stoned, that I was actually doing research for a book about the Mayan death god, didn't seem like a good idea, so I turned out my pockets for one of them while the other wandered up and down the sidewalk looking for anything I might have thrown away. They were looking for *"shit,"* apparently.

Being invited 'down to the station' was the last thing I needed so I stood perfectly still as the officer scrutinized every piece of lint from my pockets. From all reports, English cops weren't as bad as American cops[9], but *"Slip under this mattress, would you, sir, while we jump up and down on you in our big boots"* could quite easily be the method of 'interrogation' on a slow night.

After five minutes, none of the mysterious *"shit"* had materialized and the search was called off. They gave me the standard *"Fuck off and behave yourself,"* then squeezed back into the car and were gone.

I went back to my rooftops.

It wasn't as if they had nothing better to do. It was 1971. Gay militants, black militants, feminist militants, anti-Vietnam War militants were everywhere. And the Angry Brigade, which covered all the bases, was blowing up property all over England.

Confrontational revolutionary groups were a feature of the early seventies. Germany had its Baader-Meinhof gang, Italy had its Red Brigades, and England had its Angry Brigade: a group of young urban guerillas that had decided to confront the status quo head on. They'd bombed the homes of judges, high-ranking police officers, and politicians, as well as banks and army facilities. And, as an indication of feminist solidarity, they'd also blown up a 'dolly-bird' boutique in London and a BBC broadcast van in protest of The Miss World competition. Their perceived form of anarchy, which amounted to at least 25 bombs[10] so far, had now run unchecked for over a year and the police were at their wits' end trying to catch them.

When combined with the ongoing round of anti-Vietnam War demonstrations, free rock concerts, skinhead mayhem, and all-round drug taking, blowing up the place was a clear indication that the post-war baby boomers were getting out of hand.

To top things off, the *Oz* "School Kids' Issue" had just been published: *"...the most brazen and disgusting attempt to corrupt young boys and girls yet made in Britain."*[11]

The *Oz* editors had handed over one of the issues to a half-dozen teenagers and given them free rein to do whatever they wanted. The result was a criminal charge not only of producing an *"obscene article"* but of conspiring to *"corrupt the morals of young children."*

A star witness for the prosecution was England's beloved Rupert Bear, a children's comic book character who'd been around since the '20s. Rupert was (and still is) a human child with a bear's head who lived with his mum and dad and had all kinds of adventures in a place called Nutwood. His pals were also human, some with animal heads, others not.

Rupert wore plaid pants, a look that would later be adopted by punk rockers. Right now though, his pants were off. His bear's head had been pasted onto a human body drawn by Robert Crumb. Some teenage pervert had given our Rupert a woody, for God's sake!

The magazine was so innocuous, it was hardly worth buying but the resulting obscenity trial would be the longest in English history. The three editors received hefty jail sentences *and* had their hair cut off.[12]

Given the number of erections that were starting to crop up in *Ah Pook,* the event was a caution but, in the light of the trial's final outcome, not something to be concerned about. It was spring, after all. Erections were everywhere. And in case I was unfamiliar with what one looked like, Bill suggested another field trip.

He got in shape everyday with a spell in his Orgone Box, an incongruous, Tardis-like structure in his bedroom, oddly reminiscent of an outhouse.[13]

It was a homemade affair comprised of alternating layers of organic and inorganic materials — wood and metal, basically, with some rabbit fur thrown on top for good measure — with a door and a seat inside like a privy. Like a privy, the door also had a hole cut into it — to let light in, presumably, or alert others if it was already occupied. (Ideally, the subject should be naked.) The purpose of the device was to accumulate orgone, the quintessential energy named by its discoverer, Wilhelm Reich. A normal healthy flow of orgone, said Reich, was expressed through orgasm. The more flow the better.

Bill swore by its effects. Sometimes, after 20 minutes in the box, he said, he could *"Go off without even touching it."* He invited me to try.

I sat in a couple of times but, fortunately or not (the way it is when you don't have your own piano to practice on), I wasn't able to manage a spontaneous outburst.

On his advice, I'd read Reich's books, and when the documentary *WR: Mysteries of the Organism* opened, he suggested we check it out. It was the first time an erection had been shown to the general public, he said. *"It's historical!"*

The scene in question starred the Chicago Plaster Casters. A couple of art gals who'd made a career out of casting the upright cocks of rock stars. Seeing a fifteen-foot grainy hard-on on screen was a novelty, but somehow anti-climactic.

"So what did you think?" asked Bill.

"Great," I said. *"It's a start."*

Not long after, he decided to clarify what kind of "start" I might have in mind.

Writing about hard-ons, drawing pictures of hard-ons, talking about them and going to the movies to admire them made for a subtle tension that only increased as time went by. But time *did* go by and since Bill said nothing, I figured he'd simply acknowledged that I was straight and had left it at that. Unlike some of his friends, he didn't manifest any gay mannerisms at all, so most of the time it didn't even occur to me. The one-on-one older teacher/young student arrangement was new to me. Maybe a little ambiguity was normal, I thought.

He came on to me twice. Both times in the Angus Steakhouse in Piccadilly, both times when he was well lit.

We'd spend an afternoon talking, drinking, and smoking a joint maybe, and sometimes he'd suggest we eat. We'd set off in the rickety elevator, and with Bill out front in his trusty fedora, wind our way Indian file across St James's Square to the Haymarket and the Steakhouse. Once inside, his routine was invariably the same:

He placed his hat on the seat beside him, then lit up a Senior. He ordered steak, asparagus, and mashed potatoes — and a drink. When the meal arrived, he cut the meat into small pieces in the novel — and to the English, completely unacceptable — American way, with the fork clutched in his left fist. He then discarded the knife and ate with the fork like a shovel in his right, poking at the meat somewhat disinterestedly throughout the evening. The vegetables he rarely touched. Mostly he just smoked and drank.

He generally took a fresh pack of cigarettes with him when he left the flat — in case he finished the one he was working on. Senior Service 'twenties' came in a wide box. One pack fit perfectly into each pocket of his sport coat. When he emptied the first pack, rather than throw it away, he returned it to the appropriate pocket. After a few more drinks, an arrangement that led to a mesmerizing routine.

When he felt like another cigarette, without fail he first reached into the pocket containing the old pack. He pushed up the lid, discovered it was empty, and returned it to its pocket. Then he reached into the other pocket, pulled out the full pack, removed a cigarette, and lit up. A performance worthy of W.C. Fields, who Bill seemed to resemble more and more as the evening wore on. In combination with his ongoing commentary it was hypnotic — particularly when he had two cigarettes going at once.

On the evening in question, after lighting up his umpteenth, he suddenly switched to a conspiratorial tone.

"So Ma-a-a-alcolm... the Old Man of the Mountain[14] *says, 'Do as thou wilt shall be the whole of the law.'"*

"Yes, Bill..."

"So why don't we, then? We've known each other a while now."

By then his left hand had made its way to my side of the table. Kind of like a crab, I thought. My knees came together. It occurred to me we were in a steakhouse, and suddenly a whole lot was at stake.

"Well, Bill," I said, *"I guess I'll wilt."*

The crab retreated. Bill snapped back to his normal tone and sneered his 'evil' sneer.

"I was forgetting — you like gi-i-i-i-rls."

We finished the meal as if nothing had happened. Bill, as usual, ate all the complimentary Turkish Delight candy, paid the waiter, and we went our separate ways.

The second time the routine was almost identical. Including the cigarette packs and the Old Man of the Mountain. My answer was also the same.

The ambiguity it seemed, had been clarified.

Despite the lack of money, I was still able to work on other projects — also for free — all of which left me with little to show for it and all of which involved one 'Bill' or another.

The first was illustrations for *Exterminator!* Bill asked me if I would do some, so I created four black-and-white full-page images using the 'Butterflies of Fear' idea.

The fact that apprehension is described as butterflies in the stomach always seemed ironic and somehow appropriate for the work I was doing with Bill. I modified the idea for *Exterminator!* — a vaguely Mayan image of an old crone being ritualistically disemboweled by the exploding-head character I associated with Bill himself. The butterflies released contained images of Wild Boys that obliterated images of the status quo on the other three pages. Even though Bill approved and submitted them, for whatever reasons they were returned unused.

Not long after, a mysterious Canadian character named Michel Choquette showed up on Duke Street to convince Bill to contribute to a compendium of '60s celebrity comic art. He said he already had promises of material from Fellini, Frank Zappa, Robert Crumb, David Bailey, and others.

Bill felt it was a good idea and came up with a couple of *"rough"* paragraphs about electric brain stimulation.

In 1964, Professor Jose Delgado had stopped a charging bull with a transmitter. Electrodes in the bull's brain had been activated by remote control. Its aggression had effectively been switched off. *"It is the beginning of the end,"* said Bill. *"Emotion can now be triggered by a switch."*

Since this was a '60s project, I suggested the "enraged aficionados" might be '60s youth. The espontaneo could be a hermaphrodite with a bio-logic egg containing Virus B23. Bill agreed. I worked on it for a month, made a black-and-white photocopy, and handed the original to Monsieur Choquette in person. I wouldn't see or hear from either of them for 38 years.[15]

... diseased, running crowds ... bulls, hermaphrodites, biologic eggs ...

The final project was in the spring of '71.

Michael Kustow, curator of the ICA Gallery in London, invited me to contribute to an exhibition of comic art. Along with several other artists, I was asked to create an image on a four-by-eight-foot wooden panel. It was a rush job and I spent the final night at the gallery in order to make the deadline. Ralph Steadman was working on his own panel alongside. My piece was a black-and-white narrative titled *"Episode 17: Pop"*

It was part of a comprehensive show with exhibits ranging from U.S. underground artists to English children's comics. The kid's stuff though, including Rupert Bear, was pulled soon after it opened. Removed by the owners on account of, among other things, what was described in the *Times* article as a *"vulgar sex sheet"* depicting a soldier *"pricking a naked woman on the buttocks."*

That would be my panel, of course, but it would be her breast, not her buttocks. The Samurai on the horse had chased her through the swamp, caught up with her and *popped* one of her silicone implants. Certainly not the most elegant idea I'd ever had, but hardly obscene.

Despite the complaint, the gallery left the panel in place. Robert Crumb and S. Clay Wilson were also in the show but somehow managed to escape the scrutiny of the Mary Whitehouse 'morality' crowd. Maybe size did have something to do with it.

After the show, the panel was used to barricade a housing 'squat' in North London. Squatting was another aspect of early seventies counter-culture militancy: occupying vacant buildings and commandeering them as free housing. Invariably, this meant securing them against the authorities. *Episode 17: Pop* had somehow found its way to one of these buildings after the show and when the police finally broke in, was completely demolished.

So much for vulgarity.

It began to occur to me that the more time I spent around Bill Burroughs, the more the other Bill started showing up in my life. 'Brushes with the law' was taking on a whole new meaning.

... rough scenes for Ah Pook ... first layout of the book ...

In the fall, Bill decided it was time to contact his London agent. By now there were 50 pages of text.

Hieronymus Bosch's *Garden of Earthly Delights* now provided the backdrop for the final scene. The protagonists boarded the *Marie Celeste* and sailed off into the sunset. On the walls of the ruins of Hearst Castle, the graffiti read: *"Ah Pook was Here."*

I'd created character designs, sample images, and the first rough dummy of the book. We described it as a 120-page word/image novel.

Some pages would be a combination of text and image, some only text, and others entirely pictorial. It would be a combination of black-and-white and color.

A deal was signed with John Calder for publication in the UK, and, in December, a second with *Straight Arrow Books* — Rolling Stone's book division — in the US.

The total advance against royalties was $7,500 payable in three installments and split two ways. Bill and I were defined as joint authors and money and credit were to be shared 50/50. Since the third payment would be on completion, the entire amount available to produce the work was $2,500 each. I was now contractually as well as creatively committed to Bill Burroughs and *Ah Pook*.

The first check arrived in January '72... a month after my girlfriend left.

... finished art ... Hart's childhood ... Harvard... trip to the Yucatan ... discovering the lost books ... shooting Clinch Smith ... "How did this happen?"...

Saying "No" to the Old Man of the Mountain was genetically predetermined. I did like girls. I figured Bill accepted that. So when he kept up with his 'evil gi-i-i-rls' routine, I still thought it was funny.

"So Ma-a-a-alcolm," he'd say, *"What did you do this weekend? We're you with a gi-i-i-rl?"*

"Yes, Bill. I was with a gi-i-i-i-rl."

Or:

"You know the problem with gi-i-i-i-rls don't you, Malcolm?"

"What's that, Bill?"

"They get pre-e-e-egnint."

"Well, better them than us, right? I wouldn't want to have to do it."

"Uh... quite so."

I described it as the 'No girls in the treehouse routine' — a goofy, teenage boy thing. A joke. As far as I was concerned, we'd made it through the hard part and we were still working together. So what difference did it make?

... Hart's train trip back to New York ... lunar landscape of Mexico ... flesh gardens ... diseased boys ... a carnival alongside the tracks ... the gods escape from the pages ...

I'd read several of Bill's other books by now: *Junkie* (he loaned me his original Ace paperback) *The Soft Machine, The Ticket That Exploded,* and *Nova Express.* In *Dead Fingers Talk,* I discovered an interesting footnote to his sense of my having drawn him before meeting him:

When Hart shot Clinch Smith in *Cyclops,* I'd drawn him using his left hand, then posing with it afterwards in his right. An odd continuity screw up on my part, it seemed.

On page 25 of *Dead Fingers Talk,* however, Bill wrote, *"...and my left hand closed over the gun butt — I am righthanded, but I shoot with my left hand."*

Reading his books in the order they'd been written helped make his ideas more accessible, but trying to get in sync with a writing style and worldview as formidable as Bill Burroughs's was an overwhelming task. At times his ideas seemed completely impenetrable yet they alternated with pages of narrative as elegant and lucid as any I'd ever read — moments of remarkable insight that forced a determination to disentangle the rest. Bill was a *writer,* a man who worked words for all they were worth. He did so on an unprecedented scale. Coming to terms with his unique methodology while simultaneously trying to produce images that were commensurate created a learning curve like I'd never known. One that I couldn't fake, neither could I avoid. These were the most intense, far-flung ideas I would likely ever encounter. I was now legally bound as well as artistically *compelled* to understand them.

In addition to books *by* him, I also read books *about* him. Eric Mottram's *Algebra of Need* became the bible.

Then I picked up *The Job — Interviews with William Burroughs* by Daniel Odier and came face-to-face with an aspect of Bill's worldview that I was certainly not in sync with. After reading that, the 'treehouse' suddenly wasn't so funny anymore.

"Women," said Bill, *"were a basic mistake, and the whole dualistic universe evolved from that error... children are brought up by women... so that the whole human race is crippled from childhood.... Love is a fraud perpetuated by the female sex.... We aren't going to get anywhere until this ridiculous unit (the family) is disbanded."*

Etc.

And from *Minutes to Go:*

"...we went through the Ice Age in the cave and came out to hunt sickly-pale like Lazarus or any Haitian zombie with a Reactive mind[16] built in by our women who sent us. Women-sent Motherlovers to a man.

It wasn't a joke at all. He actually meant no girls on the *planet*.

Unlike the steakhouse, which made me question Bill's motives, these were ideas that made me question the integrity of the project altogether. By collaborating, I was effectively promoting an agenda which made no sense and I obviously couldn't agree with. The implications were difficult to even contemplate. Bill's wife, by this definition, had also been a "mistake." Seen in those terms, it wasn't so much a William Tell act as William *do* Tell.

Introducing my own "mistake" into the situation seemed inadvisable, to say the least. But that created a no-win situation. Girlfriend Jen may have objected to the sentiments, but she also resented being excluded from the source. The result was inevitable. It wasn't the only reason, but a year-and-a-half into the project, and five years into the relationship, she finally decided to call it quits.

Jen, as it happened, was a remarkably *beautiful* "mistake."

... Mayan city ... past time ... diseased bodies ... native workers ... a stoned priest ... Cumhu the lizard boy ... Ouab the cat ... Xolotl the Salamander ... The Painless One ... "Philde" the time-traveling drug ...

I had no method for creating imagery on this scale and no practical experience with book production. I'd been told that all books conformed to signatures, i.e. pages had to be combined in multiples of 8, 16, or 32, and based on that idea, I'd come up with 120.

To go beyond that number meant adding another signature which would amount to a more expensive book to produce and one that would take that much longer to create. To make *Ah Pook* at all practicable, therefore, I had to 'edit' the text at the start in order to come up with an overall layout. Having sketched out every scene, and combined it with the text, I then had to try and stick with it.

Bill didn't give specific directions. He might discuss a character or aspects of a scene, but I was left to my own devices for coming up with the images. Certainly with respect to the overall design. He did, ironically, make it difficult to stick with the plan.

He had no experience with a book of this nature, either, and even though he acknowledged the physical parameters, he naturally continued to add, subtract, and improve on the text the way he was used to.

Sometimes these changes were minimal, such as an additional sequence of narcotics busts: half a page of copy that amounted to maybe three more pages of imagery that could be squeezed in somehow.

Other times they weren't.

Changes like this were a problem at the rough stage. If they happened at the finished level, they were almost impossible to fix without starting over. In addition to a detailed 'realistic' style, I'd decided to make the artwork more than twice the size that it would be reproduced. A single page was 15 inches by 24 inches.

I'd started out with the same technique I'd used in *Cyclops*, but when it came to color, it didn't hold up. I tried a color wash over pen and ink but it looked too much like 'comic book' — something I'd wanted to avoid from the start.[7] Apart from the instant dismissal the word "comic" tended to evoke from publishers, *lines* around things restricted the kind of images I was able to produce — particularly with regards depth and light. They were also contrary to the very *idea* of *Ah Pook*.

The fact that the book ended up in Bosch's *Garden of Earthly Delights* led to a more realistic style, which was in keeping with my sense of Bill's writing. It had a cinematic realism to me that went beyond comic book; a romantic, boy's adventure kind of quality despite the intensity of the material.

The determining factor, though, was the Mayan imagery. In the same book that we'd discovered Ah Puch, I'd found a half-dozen black-and-white images that really impressed me. The subject matter obviously corresponded but they had exactly the kind of romantic other-worldly quality that felt right. They became the inspiration for my own.

The style of the artwork made it difficult to alter and since the text was continually subject to change, I was reluctant to commit to finished pages. Instead, I began to create frames individually with the intention of assembling them once everything was complete. This led to the idea of the book as a single image: a continuous *panorama*, something completely in keeping with the Mayan Codices.

Thinking of *Ah Pook* in this way opened up a new way of perceiving a book, and reduced the difficulties inherent in an evolving script. Most significantly, it meant I was no longer confined to a particular order when producing the images.

A true panorama is an image extended horizontally in order to achieve a complete 360-degree point of view. An image that, in effect, has no beginning or end. It was a design concept that corresponded perfectly with the ongoing, reciprocal nature of *Ah Pook*. By creating frames from whichever part of the book I felt like, I was also in sync with the concept of the book: breaking down the word/image track and traveling back and forth in time.

The book was designed to reflect the structure of a Codex with the image narrative taking place within conventional frames. When there was conflict in the story, however, this ordered structure also broke down, allowing for a free-form kind of imagery unrestrained by either frames or the edges of pages. To suggest that such chaos was always imminent, 'time holes' — irregularly-shaped sections of images from elsewhere in the book — floated randomly throughout. Mayan gods who'd escaped from Hart's books also wandered through the images both inside and outside of the frames; sometimes participating in the story, sometimes not. Mayan glyphs accompanied them, evoking Bill's notion of word as virus.

Finally, as an indication of the contrast between Hart's either/or, Judeo/Christian worldview and that of the spectral, cyclical view of the Maya, the entire book alternated between black-and-white and full color.

These were the underlying conceptual elements that were designed into the book at the outset. The surface imagery then had to be created and applied to it. Given the number of images entailed and the range of subjects Bill had come up with, this was a daunting prospect.

When the project began, the sets were minimal and there were very few characters. Now I was dealing with a huge cast, sometimes moving back and forth between time periods over the course of one or two sentences. And there was still the 'textbook' issue to contend with. Tracts of factual narrative dealing with subjects like immigration control, drug laws, and technological research that somehow had to be integrated visually with lizard boys and shrews having sex with one another.

Describing an image with text is very different from actually painting one. Words imply. A painting has to specify. In the case of a 'realistic' painting, specify every square inch. With *Ah Pook* it was an often overwhelming discrepancy.

I summed it up one time with Bill:

I said, *"If you write: 'the spaceship landed in the field and the Martian stepped out and waved,' that's fine. You've created an image in my mind that's very clear. But it's completely unspecified. If I have to make an image of the same scene, I have to figure out what kind of field it is, what time of day it is, what kind of spaceship it is, how it works, how it lands, what kind of door it has, and what the Martian looks like. I even have to figure out how long his arm is."*

Bill thought for a moment then he said, *"You're right Malcolm. So how long is a Martian's arm?"*

... Mexican guard post ... Hart with the body of Clinch Smith ... a drunk Commandante ... three bandits chosen at random then executed by firing squad ... Ah Pook's first appearance ... Los Alamos ... a Mexican bar on the moon ... American astronaut ... Mayan gods ... The baby corn god becomes Ah Pook and kills the astronaut ... Hart and the Commandante walk from the firing squad ... Modern day Mexico ... El Dia de los Muertos — The Day of The Dead ... a bandit's hat lands at the feet of a Mexican boy ... he hands it to his friend in exchange for a candy skull ... Bolivia ... high in the Andes ... The Death Academy ... Old Sarge instructs Audrey Carson and Smith's young brother Guy in the ways of dying ... the firing squad is re-enacted as an example ...

Bill was a unique storyteller. When delivered with his inimitable, authoritative drawl and sense of humor, his anecdotes made his company that much harder to resist. As anyone who has spent time with him will agree, a one-line question could often result in a long, often flawlessly worded dissertation. Given his encyclopedic knowledge and remarkable memory for quotation, there were very few subjects he couldn't hold forth on. A good memory he once said, was essential for a writer.

What made these occasions unique was that the kindly gent in the jacket and tie seemed to completely belie the intensity of the fictional imagery he generated.[18] Sitting next to him in the reverential silence of the British Museum reading room, it was difficult to reconcile his scholarly persona with time-traveling mutants being skinned alive by lobster-clawed Mayan priests — then baked inside giant metal centipedes.

In a sense he was always in character. Like Hassan-i Sabbah, the Old Man of the Mountain, or Old Sarge, handing out advice to the recruits. This often came in the form of one-liners and often out of the blue. Bill was always succinct. He talked with the same economy as he wrote. He advised the need not to talk when there was nothing to say. It was often after such periods of silence that he would throw out one of his lines, invariably on a subject completely unrelated to the one he'd previously been discussing.

On horses: *"First thing a horse thinks when you climb on it is how the fuck it's going to get you off."*

We were standing outside the British Museum while Bill smoked a Senior. We'd stopped by to look at the Aztec crystal skull that was on world tour. There were only so many times we could walk around it going: *"So whaddya think? Is it fake or is it real?"* and after a half-dozen laps, Bill decided it was time for a pit stop and some horse advice. *"They're crazy,"* he said. *"They'll run through bushes and jump off cliffs just to get you off their back."*

On transplants: *"Of course they don't work. If the body didn't want the first heart why the fuck would it want the second one?"*

He'd suddenly asked me what I thought about transplants — Christian Barnard's longest surviving patient had just died. Thinking he meant ethically or something, I said, *"If we can do it we will do it, right?"*

The irony in his response was that exactly ten years later, his son, Billy, would die of complications following a liver transplant, in a manner that clearly bore out Bill's sentiment.

On evolution: *" So how long do you suppose it takes for a cat to evolve into a rhinoceros?"*

He wasn't a fan of the slow evolutionary method. Viruses and sudden mutation were key to his view of nature — especially human nature.

In the final sequence of the book, I started to work with this idea by reintroducing extinct animals. With the possibilities of recombinant DNA — or Virus B23 — extinction really becomes a matter of being temporarily out of style. Under the right conditions, dodos and nutcracker men could be right back on set.

On space travel: " *They send a man all the way to the moon and what does he do when he gets there? Plays fucking golf!*"

He questioned the idea of sending military pilots into space.

Most of them were *religious,* for God's sake. " *If anyone prays in space, they aren't really there,*" is one of his more memorable lines. It was the substance of the astronaut's confrontation with the Mayan gods on the moon. Artists should be sent up, he said. Tell us what it *really* looks like.

On walking: *"Always look fifty feet ahead.*

Many of Bill's cautions were of a practical nature. He devoted a whole chapter to such advice in *Exterminator!*

"*D.E.,*" he called it — *Do Easy*: economy of effort in the completion of everyday chores. The sense of awareness implied in his walking rule was simply a warning to always be alert to where you are.

Many years later, he would be at the register in his neighborhood bodega in New York when he realized that the number of singles in his wallet made it look like he was loaded. He checked behind him and sure enough there was a guy he didn't like the look of. As he left the store the guy asked for his money. Old Sarge was ready for him. Like Obi-Wan Kenobi, Bill looked him in the eye and said, *"You're white, son. You don't want to rob me."* Sure enough, the guy turned and walked away.

On movies: *"Never wheel your monster on set. If you show it, you blow it."*

Science fiction was a common topic. We were talking about the fact that Stanley Kubrick had originally intended to show the aliens at the end of *2001: A Space Odyssey.* In seeming contradiction to the idea, though, Bill suggested that a truly authentic Western would be as faithful in depicting sex scenes as it would with everything else. He'd like to see John Wayne with a hard-on, for example. Full screen, 'up' there, in all its glory. See it give Katharine Hepburn a run for her money.

On writing: *"Writing is a timely business."*

He stressed the transitory nature of ideas. No matter where you were he said, the moment it occurs to you, write it down! He kept a notebook by the bed for dreams that are notoriously tenuous. I was certainly aware of that idea: I'd been drawing and writing down dreams since I was a teenager.

He also meant that ideas only manifest when the time is right.

Even if they're retained, they operate within a particular window of relevancy.

On writing: *"The purpose of writing is to make it happen."*

In our very first meeting, I'd asked Bill what *The Unspeakable Mr. Hart* was about — how did it end up? As it turned out, it *hadn't* ended up, but he'd run down some of the ingredients that might have comprised it. Underscoring all of these, he said — in fact, underscoring all writing — was its most basic intention:

"...to make it happen."

At the time, given the enormous load of new information he was handing me, I hadn't given it much thought. It was, in fact, the unique perspective that distinguished Bill Burroughs from other writers and the one that would make the biggest impression on me.

He viewed writing in terms of *effect* and questioned the inherent purpose and nature of words with respect to their capacity for achieving it.

What's in a word?

What's IN a word?

"Nobody seems to ask the question what words actually are..." he once remarked, *"...and what exactly their relationship is to the human nervous system."*[19]

He viewed them as energy — organic, even — and subjected them to laboratory-like scrutiny, relentlessly prodding at them and dissecting them to try and elicit a response — to try and determine patterns of behavior. His m.o. as a writer might be described as the process of using words to see what words can *do*.

Such an idea was unprecedented to me and truly inspiring. It placed the entire creative process within a much larger context, that went beyond 'simply' conveying a narrative idea. From this point of view, images weren't just superficial representation, either — they represented a potential more fundamental *resource*.

The image I'd drawn of Hart in response to Bill's text was a clear demonstration of *effect* and it was that event that had prompted him to pursue the interaction further. Whether or not anything else might *happen*, only time would tell, but thinking in those terms led to a very different kind of focus when making pictures. Of all his 'words of advice,' these had the profoundest *effect*.

> *... the lizard boy travels into future time ... a surreal red desert ... a deadly "Xicuitl" snake ... he steals its single egg ...*

I continued with photo reference for the characters. Now that the protagonists were young guys and young male mutants who were generally naked, I had to find models to suit. I'd sculpted the heads of the main characters for lighting reference, but I still needed the bodies to go with them. This led to surreal ongoing photo sessions: three naked straight guys in a typical London bedsit posing as lizard boys, shrews, etc. At the time, it didn't seem strange at all and as far as Bill was concerned, produced interim material that was *"very impressive indeed."* (It's interesting in retrospect, to speculate how many naked men you can have in a room before it *does* feel strange.) The models were friends of friends and they worked for free. Another idea that seemed quite normal.

Friends of their friends, in turn, were bringing up hash from Morocco. Whenever they stopped by with a fresh supply, they broke me off a chunk — also for free. I was working with Bill Burroughs, they said. I needed all the help I could get.

> *... Audrey's childhood ... a future city in chaos ... diseased faces ... Cumhu with the "fever egg" ... the crowds attack him ... he destroys them all ... orange-haired youths storm a porno store ... drag orgone machines onto the street ...*

A free supply of dope and my time to myself proved to be a very productive arrangement. A lot of work got done and it took my mind off the fact that I *was* on my own. Inevitably though, after three or four months, the routine blew a fuse, in a way that was as dramatic as it was absurd:

I ate Brillo pads.

A combination of being preoccupied with artwork and distracted by reefer resulted in steel wool being inadvertently mixed in with lunch — a situation only discovered when most of it had been eaten. (A perfectly plausible, albeit convoluted, sequence of events led to up to it. Suffice to say, I didn't just eat them straight out of the box.)

"You don't look so good," said Bill *"Are you okay, man?"*

My skin had developed a greenish tint. There were eruptions here and there. I had stomach pains and a headache that wouldn't quit.

"No," I said.

He suggested I see his private doctor on Harley Street and agreed to take care of the bill.

When I explained the situation to the good doctor, he hardly blinked.

"Are you having some sort of emotional difficulty?" he asked.

"Yes," I said.

He told me to drop my *"things"* and gave me a hefty shot of penicillin. He suggested I get some rest and *"...try not to worry."*

Then things started to blur.

For the images of Cumhu's diseased crowds, I was using the old medical books as reference. It occurred to me — as I puffed away — that such books might have been used during examinations. The doctor might have touched the patient and then touched the book, I thought. And now here I was, touching it as well...

Ten days after my visit to the good doctor, I woke up covered from head to foot in a rash.

He informed me on the phone — probably without blinking — that it was 'simply' an allergic reaction to the penicillin. He recommended I stop by the office, where he gave me a bumper shot of cortisone to take care of it. The resulting chemical stew finally brought work to a standstill. I really didn't feel good at all.

But friend Paul, who'd sneaked me into the Guy's Hospital Museum and given me the old medical books, came through once again. He showed up with a bottle of Mandrax tablets. One hundred, off the shelf, unopened. He thought they might take my mind off things.

Mandies — Quaaludes, as I'd later come to know them — were new to me. I took a few and waited for the results.

He was right. I slept for days. And as soon as I felt like they were wearing off, I took a couple more. How long it went on like that I've no idea, but very early one morning, the routine came to a halt. I was brought to my senses by somebody pulling on my big toe.

"Wakey, wakey!" announced an authoritative voice. *"You're being raided!"*

The source of the voice, a vague figure in a raincoat, then asked if I had *"...anyfink on under there?"* but without waiting for an answer, quickly pulled off the covers.

"The oldest trick in the book," said Bill. *"Hoping to catch you with an early morning hard-on."* The same old trick he'd written into *Ah Pook*. The cops would then express suitable outrage:

"What are you doing in front of decent people!?"

This particular officer was disappointed. An EMH is a fair indication of a healthy disposition. My disposition was dealing with Brillo pads.

As the room came into focus, I saw that there were five other male officers, one female — or so they'd have me believe — and two German Shepherds. The officer in charge reached down and lifted my pants from the floor. Over his shoulder, I could see the bottle of Mandrax on the bookshelf.

"Were you intendin' to wear *these?"* he asked.

"Yes," I said.

After searching in vain for pockets to rifle through, he threw them at me with obvious distaste and told me to get up.

Only women wear pants without pockets, of course. His reaction was understandable. But these were definitely men's pants.

I'd made them myself.

Alan, the flatmate and Led Zeppelin fan, had shown me how to do it. Why not? They were cheap and you could make them out of anything you wanted.

In this case, I'd opted for a broad striped alternating dark blue/bright blue upholstery fabric with yellow pinstripes. Something probably intended for deck chairs. Apart from the lack of pockets and discrepancies in the fit (this was my first attempt), they also had an added feature created by the fabric itself: being 100% polyester, after a couple of days' wear, the knees and backside retained the contours from the sitting position. Meaning, when I was standing, they stuck out front and back quite significantly. Nevertheless, I'd been sufficiently proud of my achievement to debut them in a visit to Duke Street.

"Nice pants," said Bill.

"Thanks," I said. *"I made them myself."*

"I can see that," he said.

I took it as a caution and from then on only wore them around the house. Now chock full of downers and Brillo, I put them on once more to confront the powers that be. It would be all that I'd be wearing during the event.

The moment I had them zipped up, the officer in charge smiled, turned, reached for the mandies and swung them around in front of my face.

"And what might these be, then?"

"On prescription from Doctor Fitzgibbon-Wright of Harley Street," I said without missing a beat. *"I've not been well..."*

In England, a doctor on Harley Street with a double-barreled name can work wonders. There was a pause — then the bottle went back on the shelf. At which point the raid began in earnest.

It *was* research, so I paid close attention.

As if a whistle had been blown, the dogs went after my cat, the 'woman' went after the dogs, and the men went rummaging haphazardly around the room. Given that it was a small bedsit, once you took six large coppers, an equally large woman, two dogs, me, a bed, drawing table, light table, and other furniture into account, the rummaging was somewhat limited.

After ten minutes they hadn't found anything. Not even in the couple of porno magazines they'd each searched through thoroughly in turn.

It was my first raid, so I was unsure what was supposed to happen next. When everyone just stood around and chatted, I assumed it was normal.

One enterprising bobby, trying to make conversation — or possibly thinking he might trick me — pointed to the Ah Pook artwork and asked if I'd done it.

"Yes," I said, thinking I had an admirer.

"It's very good," he said, *"but it's a bit sick. What do you use to do some-thing like that?"*

"Oh, you know, inks, pencils, acrylics," I says.

"No, no, no," he says, all conspiratorial-like. *"What do you u-u-use?"*

What do **you** 'u-u-use', I thought, to drag people out of bed in the morning?

Since there was no answer forthcoming from either of us, he stepped back with the rest, who continued to mutter amongst themselves.

Thinking it might be part of the protocol, I asked if they'd like a cup of tea or something — I was going to make some anyway. The officer in charge actually looked at his watch to consider.

"No thank you, sir. We've got a couple hundred more busts to make."

When I asked what had *"occasioned such an intrusion"* (I was awake now), he replied, *"The 'ighest court in the land would not be able to make me di-vulge that information, sir."*

And then: *" A mate tipped us off."*

At which point the entire group about-faced and filed out into the hall. As he was leaving he turned and gave me one last cryptic piece of advice: *"Don't keep the shit on the premises!"*

I made a note of it. Along with the first quote for the back of the book: *"It's very good, but it's a bit sick."* — The London Metropolitan Police

To describe things as blurred seemed apt. There was indeed a bust in *Ah Pook*. Bill had written it in the year before:

> *"Narcs rush in...they look around in disgust...*
> *"And they call us animals..."*
> *"Dirty books...dirty pictures..."*
> *A narc has found a bottle of laudanum...*
> *"AND DOPE"...He holds up the bottle his eyes shining..."*

In the book or out of the book here, Bill?

Bill found it highly amusing. Saying it was a mate tipped them off was *also* the oldest trick in the book, he said. My friends suggested the reason might have been the Angry Brigade.[20]

Scotland Yard had been trying to catch them for almost two years and had been raiding people's homes all over London. I was told they'd gone through the names in the rolodexes of underground magazines looking for possible 'suspects.' Ostensibly, they were searching for evidence of terrorism. In fact, they had carte blanche to enter homes and uncover things that had nothing to do with it. For the officers involved it was also an opportunity for a bit of fun. It explained why they'd hung around so long.

My other flatmate, Richard across the hall, had also been visited. When he told them he needed to use the bathroom, the two officers went with him. They'd spent ten minutes sitting side-by-side on the bathtub, their knees touching his, as he sat facing them on the toilet. Acting on a hunch, presumably that he'd gone to bed the night before with explosives hidden up his backside.

It was only in retrospect that these things were funny. At the time, I'd felt the same combination of comedy and terror that I had on acid. Saying the wrong thing or doing the wrong thing could have had me "down the station" just for the hell of it. Not something I wanted at that time of the day — especially wearing those pants. Things might have been very different if the officer in charge had noticed there was no prescription label on the Mandrax. Or if the dogs hadn't been so busy with the cat that they'd seen the hash pipe on the floor. Or if the artwork on the drawing table had been the end of Cumhu's trip instead of the beginning:

> *... the orange-haired youths aim the orgone machines at the crowd ... people tear their clothes off and fuck on the sidewalk, in doorways, and taxi cabs ... cops and ambulance attendants among them ... humping and heaving around the statue of Eros ...*

It's one of my favorite *Ah Pook* images but unfortunately — or fortunately — it never made it past the rough stage. Bill hadn't specified in his text that the orgy participants would transition to disease, but since the trip had started with diseased running crowds it seemed appropriate.

Changing the billboards into sex scenes also made sense. These were based on the actual ads in Piccadilly Circus at the time. Those for jewelry, alcohol, and makeup, in particular, promoted sex as the reason for buying the product, so I figured why not cut to the chase and show folks getting down to their just rewards. "Max Factor for Charm" implies what, after all? Charm in order to achieve what?

Even though this is unquestionably the implication, representing it explicitly is considered pornography. Which is the obscene duplicity of censorship: you can point at the sex act every which way, but you can't actually show it. It's against the law. The law of the *market,* that is.

"*Never wheel your monster on set. If you show it, you blow it.*"

It took a while for the chemical stew to subside. Bill suggested acupuncture might help.

He'd run into an eccentric medical character who claimed to have learned it from a "*...Chinaman during the war.*" Which war, he didn't say. It was very effective, said Bill. He set up an appointment for me and once again agreed to pay. It was to be my first experience with 'alternative' medicine.

Acupuncture itself is surreal. The 'doctor' — an elderly gent who was apparently practicing in his living room — made it that much more so.

Having introduced ourselves, we sat on either side of his cluttered desk and he briefly explained the procedure. He would be inserting several needles into various parts of the body at once he said, some of which

— given my condition — might hurt. It should take about a half an hour, he said. He studied me intently as he spoke.

Since I had no questions, he then led me over to the examination table at the back of the room and told me to get undressed. Down to your underpants, he said, then climb up and get comfortable.

As I handed him my clothes, he asked if his friend might observe. I said I had no objection and the friend instantly materialized beside him. From where exactly was unclear. He then pulled a curtain around us — for privacy, presumably — and the both of them considered their patient. This first visit would be diagnostic, said the doctor, to determine where my strengths and weaknesses lay.

After several moments of scrutiny, he produced a small flat tobacco tin in which he kept the needles steeped in alcohol. Very professional, I thought — a sentimental object, perhaps — from the war maybe. Most of the needles hurt when they were inserted and when it came time to tweak the meridians, I decided it would probably be my last visit. The doctor explained the reasons for the jolts and suggested we set up another appointment to deal with them. His silent, nodding assistant concurred.

I got dressed, thanked them for their time, and left. How much it cost, Bill didn't say. The two gentlemen seemed to have enjoyed themselves. Maybe that was payment enough.

Bill next suggested a few sessions with the 'cans.'

He'd referred to the Scientology E-meter several times and one afternoon when I showed up at Duke Street, John McMaster, an apparent expert with the device, was there to meet me. McMaster was a handsome, soft-spoken man about the same age as Bill who had the distinction of being Scientology's first 'Clear.' Like Bill, he'd left the church in response to its founder's controlling methods — something the church wasn't happy with. They'd since tried to kill him, said John. We sat across from one another at the conference table, the small wooden box and cans between us.

The E-meter functions like a lie detector. The 'cans' (literally tin cans) are held in order to relay the galvanic response that occurs during the process of questioning. From these 'reads' on the meter it's possible to identify ideas that are emotionally 'charged' in the subject's mind. In Scientology, the process is called auditing. Its purpose is to neutralize the issues of concern and bring the meter needle to rest — to render the subject 'clear'.

A full audit is a long, intense, and expensive procedure involving trained auditors operating with very specific interrogating methods. John simply gave me an idea of the way the process worked.

For 30 minutes he asked me alternately:

"What is a condition of existence?"

"What is not a condition of existence?"

Being forced to come up with a different answer each time inevitably led to an examination of both the question and the meaning and emphasis of each of the words that comprised it. By repeatedly questioning the opposing consideration of the same idea, I came up with many unexpected personal insights, the emotional scale of which could clearly be seen on the meter.

Regardless of the shrink value, the process of interrogating an idea in terms of its opposite in this way was clearly a valuable creative tool.

The second session was at my place and it wasn't so simple.

John removed the E-meter from his bag and decided to set up on my bed. We sat on either side with the device between us.

The questions this time were:

"Who is someone you have known?'

"Who is someone you have not known?"

Questions that inevitably led to more personal revelations.

One of them was my best friend, Tony, who'd drowned when he was 7 years old. The fact that he was my age and that he'd drowned in the river where we swam together naturally had a profound effect on me. I remember standing on the riverbank many times after that, peering at the spot where it had happened. The water was clear there, almost invisible, yet it had held him down and killed him.

The memory got a big read. John suggested we focus on it. I happened to mention that Tony and I had jerked off together a few times. This seemed very significant to John. He suggested another session.

It didn't feel right at all. What exactly was I being cleared of here? I decided to give needles a rest.

... the lizard boy confronts his father ... an old man metamorphosizing into an insect ... You must punish yourself, he says ... you have been indulging in "extreme experience" ... you must "draw the thorns." Cumhu tells him to draw thorns through his own prick and kills him ... he steals the sacred books, enabling him to move into future time ...

The gay thing was starting to wear thin. "No" for an answer apparently wasn't good enough. Bill had once said that feminists accused him of being a *"male colonizer."* He'd asked if I agreed with them. At the time I didn't understand what he meant. From my point of view I was a straight kid and he was a gay man. A distinction that was hardwired. From his point of view, I was a guy who just needed to be convinced he was wrong. *"You'd have a great career as a homosexual,"* he said.

The fact that I was drawing naked 'guys' all day didn't help. And not being able to find another 'mistake' to fill the emotional void made it hard to shrug it off. The "gi-i-i-irls" routine definitely wasn't funny anymore.

Then the advance money ran out. I had to look for bullshit freelance work. As a backdrop, I had the entire memorized text of *Ah Pook* running through my head: gay sex, fear, death, disease, and the end of the world. Day and night.

Making images wasn't a matter of turning on a faucet every day and having it happen. It was subject to a kind of internal weather as unpredictable and unalterable as real weather. Sometimes there were lulls when nothing moved at all, then there were times when the energy was there but the images produced were atrocious. What was acceptable, ultimately, was the quality of imagery achieved when all the right elements were working together. Anything short of that was not. Right now, things weren't working at all.

I finally decided to talk to Bill about it.

His response was the last thing I wanted to hear. It came straight from the 'treehouse.'

"So Ma-a-a-lcolm. Did ya slap her?"

"Slap her?"

"You know what Humphrey Bogart used to say — 'I never met a woman yet who didn't respond a whole lot better looking up from the floor.'"

Whether Humphrey Bogart actually said it or not, I never bothered to find out. The following week I signed on for the dole at the Willesden Labour Exchange, stopped working on *Ah Pook,* and stopped talking to Bill. Then I stopped making art altogether.

The workload was bad enough. That and the lack of money. I didn't need this crap as well. I finally just said fuck it to all of it. In his own words: *"...you can't write unless you want to write, and you can't write if you don't feel like it."* Same with images, Jack. He called several times, even showed up at the flat, but I didn't answer. Ah Pook wasn't here.

I spent the next few months basically doing nothing. The dole kept me afloat and my private detective buddy, Phil, provided the beer money. His wife had just left him so we had that in common. She'd thrown his suit into the bathtub to get back at *him* for something. He'd chopped down the bedroom door with an axe to get at *her*. Relationships were fucked.

We spent the time driving around the country, hanging out, smoking reefer, listening to the police radio. If there was a robbery in progress, he'd use his reverse phone directory to call the address and tip the crook off. There were a few people out looking for Phil. He carried a hammer in his briefcase on that account.

"Where the fuck do you hit someone with a hammer and not kill them?"

"On the elbow, mate. On the elbow."

It was the real thing. None of that art shit.[21]

Then I met a woman on a subway and everything went downhill. She was living with a rock musician but I was determined. Followed her all over England, even. Way up in Southport, I finally talked to her on the phone. Her boyfriend had won some kind of lottery, she said. They'd gotten married and she was pregnant.

Phil and I got drunk and drove the car out onto the beach. When the tide suddenly came in, we tried to push it back. That's when the ass of the homemade pants finally gave out. It was the end. What was the point of *anything*?

By the end of the year, I'd had 'enough,' enough. I wanted out *completely*. But then one night around 11:00, like a light switch being flipped, everything turned around. The way it is, she came out of nowhere. Jump start. Problem solved.

Katharine.

I started freelance work again. We went to Europe together, traveled around England, and went looking for mushrooms in Wales. The mushrooms were a bust, but while I was there I took my first photographic panoramas: reference images for the backdrop to a vigilante scene in *Ah Pook*. It was apparently time to get back to work. I called Bill when I got home to see where we stood.

His immediate reaction was understandable. He clarified that it was I who'd broken off communication. His explanation for my doing so, though, was both a revelation and a vindication. It was on account of my last session with John McMaster, he said. By recalling my childhood, I'd been confronted with proof of my own *"latent homosexuality — and couldn't handle it."*

How about that? I thought. I'd been tag teamed. Where do we go from there?

As it happened, regardless of what I thought of their prognosis, once it had been pointed out to me, remarkably, everything changed. From then on, there would be no more tension, no more mention of gi-i-i-irls, and no more Old Man of the Mountain. One way or another, the issue had finally been resolved. We could get on with the book.

We decided to talk to Straight Arrow before we went any further to find out what kind of production issues were involved. The only way to determine that was by sending them the artwork, so in September of that year we mailed everything to San Francisco.

Their response was to have me come to them and explain what they were looking at.

With that in mind, there was one piece of research I needed to take care of. I arranged a trip to the Bisley shooting range in Surrey with a friend and spent a Sunday afternoon shooting as many kinds of guns as possible. Members exchanged with one another and I became familiar with a Winchester rifle, Civil War Navy Colt, .38 Special, and .357 Magnum, among others. If Bill's own preoccupation with guns was at all typical, it seemed wise to at least be aware of the procedure.

Bill had moved now to another flat in the building. Unlike the one he'd shared with Brion, it was small and claustrophobic. Adding to the feeling was Johnny — his new live-in partner. Johnny "The Sailor" as he described himself, an Irish kid about the same age as me. He didn't talk much. It wasn't his forte. He usually left when I arrived.

Bill had once remarked that sex wasn't a time for laughter. I'd wondered what that kind of sex would be like. Johnny Brady seemed to offer a clue.

A couple of weeks before I left for America, Bill offered to cook dinner. The sailor had gone ashore so it was just the two of us. He set the plates, then busied himself in the kitchen alcove, finally emerging with a small saucepan from which he ladled a mound of broad beans onto each plate. After we'd finished, he asked if I'd care for more. He returned to the alcove, then reappeared several minutes later with another saucepan. This time full of *baked* beans.

That was it. One of the most memorable meals I've ever had.

SAN FRANCISCO

I arrived the day after Halloween: Día de los Muertos.

It was my first trip to America and a U.S. Immigration official at the airport welcomed me personally. He insisted I accompany him to his office and explain my reasons for being there. I described *Ah Pook* to him briefly and showed him the contract with Straight Arrow. I could have recited the entire book but it seemed inappropriate:

"How many times will you compulsively repeat the explanation you have ready in case the customs official starts asking questions?"

He was *"mighty impressed"* that a *"young fella"* like me would be paid *"so much money"* to write a book. He wished me luck and sent me on my way.

The people at Straight Arrow had unaccountably determined ahead of time that I was gay and middle-aged. Accordingly, they'd arranged a room at The Press Club (not that those were the qualifications for membership). The sedate literary atmosphere was presumably considered appropriate.

The next morning, early, I walked to the office. There were *streetcars* and *cable cars* but I had no idea where they went or how to use them. I passed a bank with a *stagecoach* for a logo and another building shaped like a *pyramid*. I was actually here.

I reviewed the artwork with editor-in-chief Alan Rinzler and we agreed that I should go back to England, collect whatever materials I needed, then return in the New Year to finish the job. We reckoned it would take six months.

Then I wandered back to the Press Club.

Fortunately, the assistant art director of *Rolling Stone*, Dian Ooka, found me a sublet in an artist's loft downtown. I was able to work there and, in addition to the painters and sculptors in the building, also started to meet other artists in the city.

... The Garden of Earthly Delights ... mutants ...

I got back in February. The initial shock had worn off and I was able to get a better sense of my surroundings. The country was in a state of depression, apparently.

The Vietnam War was going badly, the Watergate tapes had just been released, "serial killer" had become an official genre. Ted Bundy was getting started up in Washington state and San Francisco had its very own Zebra Killer. Reflecting the mood, the first 'slasher' movie had appeared. *The Texas Chain Saw Massacre* together with the *Exorcist* had raised cinematic violence to new heights.

And Elvis had doubled in size.

The locals were coming to terms with it in all manner of ways. Zen guru Alan Watts was on the radio day and night. *Est* was everywhere, along with Arica, transcendental meditation, rolfing, and gestalt. John and Yoko were encouraging folks to scream their hearts out. Maharishis, swamis, and babas were wading ashore in droves.

Straight Arrow agreed to pay the second installment of the advance. Bill generously gave me his share. The loft was no longer available so I found myself an apartment on Nob Hill. A small one-bedroom, furnished with a mattress, homemade drawing table, the wooden box I'd shipped my stuff in, and a chair.

... Percy Jones and the Whisperer ... 1930s imagery ... mutants ... the Garden of Delights ... Vigilantes ... Reddies ...

Maxfield Parrish and San Francisco poster art inspired me to work on character sketches for the Garden of Delights end sequence and my new digs at 1420 Jones Street had me unconsciously working on *Percy Jones*. Trips to Muir Woods and Mount Tamalpais prompted me to complete the vigilante scene I'd begun before I left England. It was all on the wall when my first official visitors showed up.

San Francisco also had its own Angry Brigade: The Symbionese Liberation Army. A couple of days after I arrived, they kidnapped newspaper heiress Patty Hearst.

In April, she helped them rob a San Francisco bank. In May, a SWAT team gunned down leader Donald DeFreeze and five other members in Los Angeles. Patty wasn't among them. The San Francisco cops and the FBI stepped up the search, encouraging people to report unusual characters moving into their neighborhoods.

A couple of days later they showed up at my place.

Nob Hill was a fairly respectable area, but I was surprised that somebody considered *me* worth a call. Maybe it was the odd hours I kept. I preferred working at night. When the downstairs doorbell rang around lunchtime, I was still in bed.

Since very few people knew where I lived, I buzzed in whoever it was and waited at the apartment door in my bare feet.

As the two men came up the stairs it occurred to me they might be Jehovah's Witnesses. I was struck by the plaid pants. Not something you see very often in England.

"FBI," announced one of them.

Especially on a police officer.

They came in, arranged themselves side-by-side beside the door and flipped their badges. Reference material, I thought. I leaned in for a closer look.

"We're making enquiries about the Patty Hearst kidnapping," said one of them. *"Have you seen any strange or unusual people in the building lately?"*

A tricky question under the circumstances.

"No," I said.

He handed me a stack of about 30 black-and-white photographs, about the size of baseball cards, secured with a rubber band. Mostly pictures of black guys.

"Have you seen any of these people?" he asked.

Things were beginning to blur. I explained that I'd only just arrived in San Francisco but he insisted I look anyway.

"Well this is Donald DeFreeze," I said. *"He's dead."*

"That's OK," he said, *"just keep looking."*

Which I did, until his partner suddenly pointed to the wall above my drawing table and announced: *"That's Patty Hearst's grandfather! And so's that! And that's Hearst Castle. And...."*

And he was right. There were also pictures of cops, terrorists, atomic bombs, and dead people. And replica guns on the table.

When I looked back they were both reaching for the hips of those pants.

It was an odd sensation. Two versions of a similar idea were in the same room together; one real, one imaginary. The cops were part of the real part and so were the guns. But then again, even that was strange. I was English. Cops with guns were something I'd only read about, or seen in the movies. And I'd *never* seen cops in plaid pants. It was like a dream. For a moment I didn't feel like I was anywhere at all.

"What exactly do you do?" asked one of them.

"I'm an artist," I said, *"working on a book... based on Randolph Hearst... Randolph Hearst senior... a kind of science fiction story... by William Burroughs... he wrote it years ago..."*

There was a beat, then the moment passed. The idea went its separate ways. The hands came off the pants.

One of them pointed to the Ah Pook artwork — the picture of the vigilantes running through the woods.

"What's happening there?" he asked.

"It's a time in the future," I said, *"when law and order breaks down."*

He studied it for a while then turned to me with a concerned, knowing look.

" Frightening," he said.

As they left, he handed me an FBI wanted poster. Of the five people shown, only one was still alive — Patty Hearst.

"If you see any of these people let us know," he said.

At this point anything's possible, I thought.

There was no cryptic advice this time, but I did have a second quote for the back of the book:

"Frightening" — The FBI

The fact that Bill had chosen Randolph Hearst as the model for the instrument of Control was uncanny. The crisscrossing of real and imagined events however, was far more complex and more eerily profound.

The media portrayed the SLA as an army of young radicals confronting the status quo — reminiscent of the boy heroes in *Ah Pook*. In fact, it was the opposite: the idea turned against itself. An entity created *by* the Control Machine, designed to undermine legitimate protest — particularly Black protest — invoking fears of random murder, robbery, and kidnapping. A justification for escalating military and legislative assault on all forms of dissent.

By setting DeFreeze up with an 'army' of smart young attractive *white* women, Control stirred up a Reactive Mindset accessing fears of sex, race, and violence.

As Bill put it in *Ah Pook* years before:

"The Black Fever attacks the sexual centers and the centers of sensitization

producing a massive reaction as if the victim had been attacked by a swarm of killer bees..."

Nothing upsets John Q. Citizen more than thinking some other guy is getting a better shake of the stick, especially if it's with several young women at once. And especially if he's a *black* guy. A black guy with an armed harem of white "love slaves" committing acts of robbery and violence on his behalf. The ultimate aim of which — according to the media — was an insurrectionary army intent on similar acts of violence and mayhem across America.

> *"Through his newspapers Mr. Hart appeals to the silent majority.*
> *'THE NIGGERS IS KILLING OUR WOMEN FOLK'*
> *Vast patriotic rallies are organized."*
>
> — *Ah Pook is Here*

The intersection of fact and fiction was certainly noteworthy but compounding the scenario was a book published two years previously, a book that not only read like a blueprint for the actual events but also manifested the same kind of phenomenon.

Black Abductor, published in 1972,[22] is a novel in which a group of campus revolutionaries headed by a young black guy, kidnap the daughter of a prominent conservative politician to use as a hostage. The political scenario is almost identical to that surrounding Patty Hearst and is astutely written. Police and media reaction and the implications of hostage taking as a revolutionary strategy in the United States is convincing to the point that it essentially runs down the way the real kidnapping would unfold:

The victim is a rich white female college student.

She's abducted at night while she's with her boyfriend, who's badly beaten.

She's kept in a house close to the crime.

She has sex with her captors and becomes a convert to their political ideology.

Her name is *Patricia*.

In the book or out of the book?

Black Abductor filled in the blanks ahead of time about what it might have been like for the real Patricia. A concern that featured as the prurient subtext during the event: not so much that she was being brainwashed, but the nature of thing that was doing the washing.

The political intrigues serve as backdrop for explicit sex scenes in which the leader's prodigious member essentially becomes the means for political indoctrination. And the young heiress, once she overcomes her initial fearfulness and realizes that her vagina can withstand the pressure, is consumed by an insatiable need to *know* more. As Bill had put it long ago: *"No question about the star of the show."*[23]

But who would read such a book? It doesn't work as conventional porno because the ideas are too intellectual. And it doesn't work as political commentary because it's full of blowjobs and throbbing clitorises.

Whatever it was, or how it was connected to subsequent events will probably never be known. The FBI conducted a "thorough search" for the writer and the publisher but was unable to find either. If the book had been truly prophetic, it seems more likely the author wouldn't *need* to be found. He would have probably jumped at the opportunity for recognition. Instead, the government tracked down a porno writer in California named Harrison James who denied he'd written it. They left it at that. Case closed. Whatever its provenance, appropriately it smelled fishy.

As a final thread in the entanglement, in 1976 another Berkeley underground group — Tribal Thumb — issued a communiqué during the trial of Patty Hearst. It essentially ran down the government's involvement and the Hearsts' complicity in the SLA, and incorrectly made reference to a book titled *Vanished, "published by a publishing company named Nova owned by the Hearst Corporation."* Ever since his book, *Nova Express*, Bill kind of had dibs on the word.

Books *within* books... wheels within wheels...

My next official visitor on Jones Street was Jann Wenner, owner of *Rolling Stone* and Straight Arrow Books. He'd decided to check on the status of the project in person. He was impressed with what he saw, but was more interested in how long it would take to finish it. I was unaware at the time that he was considering closing Straight Arrow down. *Ah Pook is Here,* as an expensive-to-produce work in progress, naturally factored in the mix.

I kept working regardless.

... duo-tone tests of Percy Jones, Audrey and the Dib ... hand lettering ...

David Charlesen, *Straight Arrow's* publishing consultant, helped devise ways to cut production costs. He suggested 'duotone' as an alternative to full color. The technique would reduce the amount of time necessary to create the artwork, since everything would be created in black-and-white and save money in reproduction since only two colors were involved.

I also worked with calligrapher friend Mark Behrens to create a hand-drawn style for the text. This seemed more in keeping with the original codex. Mark designed a lettering style to reflect the character of the glyphs and then transposed Bill's narrative at the same scale as the images. This amounted to sheet after sheet of copy, written in a consistent style, without a mistake. No mean accomplishment.

Bill had suggested I look up a friend of his named Bill Belli. Bill had met Bill in Paris during his student days and he was now a practicing lawyer in San Francisco. (Ten years in the future, his photograph would be used on the cover of Ted Morgan's biography, *Literary Outlaw: The Life and Times of William S. Burroughs*.) Bill and his wife Marjorie fed the starving artist many times. On one occasion, Bill Burroughs, Jr. showed up with his wife, Karen. More Bills than you could shake a stick at.

Billy Jr. was a chubby guy the same age as me, unlike his father in every way. He sat on the floor the entire time and held forth with a barely audible, machine-gun-like delivery — pausing once in a while to light another cigarette or chastise his wife for interrupting. He'd lit incense alongside himself for the occasion. Demeanor and appearance aside, he was a very accomplished writer and signed and gave me the copy of *Kentucky Ham* he had with him. I knew next to nothing about him. Bill had mentioned that he *had* a son but that was all. It was a short visit. I wouldn't see him again for five years.

I'd continued working on the vigilante scene because David Charlesen had suggested I complete the expensive full-color work first. This included character designs for the scenes beyond that, including mutants in human skin suits.

The Mayan priests sometimes flayed their sacrificial victims and slipped into the skins as an added perk to the proceedings. I extended the concept to include characters from earlier in the book being transformed into a kind of apocalyptic fashion statement later on. Some of Percy Jones's detractors, who wear fur coats, are transformed in this way. Two such dapper mutants, standing in front of a defaced Mayan wall, were to be on the cover of the book.

Bill was living in New York by this time. In the spring, he flew out for a visit. He brought the colored pencils I'd asked for, plus a new traveling companion; a deferential young guy, a couple of years younger than me — also in a jacket and tie — named James. He didn't say much. I didn't see much of him.

Bill brought S. Clay Wilson by to show him the Ah Pook artwork and the three of us spent the afternoon together in the revolving bar of the Hyatt Regency. Both sported fedoras and since it was his birthday, S. Clay wore a natty three-piece suit complete with pocket watch and chain. Like a couple of Chicago gangsters, it occurred to me, talking pirates, dykes, and mayhem.

Bill and I also went to movies together. *Chinatown* was playing way out on Geary and we arrived a half-hour early. After a couple of Seniors outside, Bill finally said, *"What the heck. Let's just go in. What difference will it make?"*

As we took our seats we heard:

"She's my sister! ... She's my daughter! ... She's my sister and my daughter!"

We also ate together.

Bill, James, Mark Behrens, a young punk/glam rocker *"ripped on downers,"* and I got together for a Mexican meal at Mario's on Bush Street — an event worthy of a fairly long entry in one of my journals. John Giorno, a poet from New York, also joined us.

Bill, who was already quite merry, described his *"catch for the night"* as *"a character from one of my books"* and sat directly across from him. Halfway into the meal, I heard a familiar refrain:

"So, David! The Old Man of the Mountain says, 'Do as thou wilt shall be the whole of the law'..."

This time he hit pay dirt. The kid — who'd complained all night about being bored — suggested the two of them go to an orgy.

Bill said *"Yes!"* immediately and off they went — the kid tottering ahead on his platform shoes, a well-lubricated Bill in hat, jacket, and tie weaving deliberately and determinedly behind.

In the summer of '74, Straight Arrow finally closed up shop. Right around the time Nixon resigned. They offered *Ah Pook* to Simon and Schuster but, being straighter than Straight, Simon and Schuster declined. I was stuck without a publisher, without a job, and with no money.[24]

By September, the situation had become precarious enough to warrant a letter of desperation to agent Peter Matson.

My telephone was about to be cut off, my visa about to expire, and if last month's rent wasn't forthcoming within a week, I'd be out on the street. Not to mention, as I put it, *"...although possibly an incidental,"* I hadn't had any money in two months and had nothing to live on. I sent a copy of the letter to Bill and, generous as ever, he mailed me a personal check for $300 right away.

Under the circumstances, I had more pressing concerns, but Bill's cover letter revealed a strange new departure in our working relationship — It was written by the new traveling companion, James. For the first time it was *"we"* who had received my letter. The reply included such phrases as: *"Both William and I...* and *"evidence of our sincerity..."*

James added that he *"endorsed"* my position and enclosed Bill's money. *"I hope it keeps you off the streets...."*

He concluded, *"As ever, James."*

It was an interesting development, but right now I had more important things to worry about. Divvying up 300 bucks to pay off debts and still have enough to live on was absurd. I needed *money.*

True to form, *Ah Pook* came through again. It was already written in: that month I got a job with the army.

The most substantial addition to the original text had been an episode where Old Sarge and the young recruits had traveled back in time to the island of Queimada,[25] getting there ahead of William Walker and the British in order to set up an ambush. It had been impossible to fit it into the already-laid-out dummy so it wasn't included. In the preparations for the attack, Bill had included four pages of detailed instructions on how to assemble and deploy weaponry.

Consistent with that idea, I ended up on the island of Alameda, creating detailed instructions for young U.S. army recruits — on how to assemble and deploy weaponry.

Each lesson was broken down into a series of steps, each step being an image with the relevant instruction. Within six months, in the course of producing hundreds of images for the GIs, I'd learned how to set up field telephones and radar scanners, repair tanks and other vehicles, align artillery gunsights, break down and clean personal weapons, attend to injuries — including amputations — and camouflage vehicles and personnel.

In deference to a much *larger* future already planned, as per instruction, I'd switched the camouflage colors from 'jungle' to 'desert.'

The army job was freelance, so I was able to work from home and continue with *Ah Pook*.

Bill was scheduled to give a reading in the Bay Area in November of '74 and as a lead-up to the event, the *Berkley Barb* featured a four-page centerspread,[26] including a comic strip by S. Clay Wilson. The paper interviewed Allen Ginsberg about Bill and I donated my four illustrations from *Exterminator!* to accompany it. The *Barb* printed them all on the same page and paid me a hundred bucks.

The article itself was chopped by a bad paste-up artist, but what was more disquieting was Ginsberg's deadly serious reference to Bill's *"late theory"* that Earth was in the thrall of a viral invasion from Venus. Not from other galaxies anymore — but *"an extraterrestrial threat from within our own solar system."* Was somebody pulling somebody's leg here?

... Audrey, The Dib and Jimmy the Shrew ... Jimmy fucks Audrey in return for two Walther P38s ...

My brief encounters with Bill Junior and James inspired work on a sequence that takes place in Palm Beach. Billy was raised there by his grandparents and The Dib introduces Audrey to Jimmy the Shrew there. It was another Ah Pook sequence that didn't get past the rough stage and much of what there was of it would be eaten by bugs.

The model for Audrey changed several times during the project. Initially, Bill had produced a small snapshot of a young guy he'd met in Switzerland named John de Chadenedes and told me his was the face he had in mind. It was woefully inadequate for what I needed, so my youngest brother Kevin posed for the reference pictures in England, followed by Felon Black and then Mike Tebb. When I arrived in San Francisco I tried contacting de Chadenedes who, according to Bill, was living on Polk Street at the time, but I was unable to find him. As a last resort, I ended using pictures of myself. I was now officially in the book.

In November, the army insisted I work on the premises, meaning I had to commute back and forth across the Bay Bridge in rush hour every day. Any other work was out of the question. A month or two later, when they discovered I didn't have a green card, they fired me — but then offered to sponsor one if I agreed to work for them for two years. It sounded a lot too much like 'barracks' to me, so I quit. I had some money now but I still needed to sort out that particular problem. I decided to talk to a lawyer.

I had a thousand dollars in cash and a letter from Mr. William S. Burroughs insisting that I be allowed to stay in the country. How could he refuse? The lawyer studied both and smiled.

"Forget it," he said.*" Get lost... or get married."*

I bought a two-hundred-and-fifty dollar Chevy and did both.

NEW YORK

1975

I drove across the George Washington Bridge in May '75. Disco was on the radio, the Watergate gang was in jail. The Vietnam War had ended just days before and Pol Pot, an entirely other form of serial killer, was getting started in Cambodia. In a couple of months, Patty Hearst would be found and Jimmy Hoffa would disappear. Gerald Ford would gain the dubious distinction of being the only president in American history — or any other history, for that matter — to be shot at twice by women. *Global cooling* and the fear of a new ice age would have scientists ready to dump soot on the Arctic ice cap.

I had 900 bucks. If I liked it here, I'd stay. If not, I'd just keep going. Back to where I'd come from.

Friend Ernie had an empty sublet on Houston Street and I moved in. Bill was living at 77 Franklin Street, a few blocks south, in an area called Tribeca.

Converting industrial buildings into living spaces was only beginning back then and at night, an area where lofts now cost millions of dollars was a deserted no-man's land. There were no stores open, few lights, and, if you were lucky, you might see the one cop car that patrolled all the way to the end of the island. The first time I visited Bill was at night, and when I came up out of the subway, the neighborhood seemed so desolate I thought I was in the wrong place.

I called from the corner payphone — the way you did back then — and waited nervously for him to let me in. It took a while. Some lofts had elevators; this was a walk-up. Bill lived on the top floor. The building had been there since the 1860s. The stairs were original.

The loft was sparsely furnished, wooden floor worn from years of industrial use. A five-foot square white field painting by David Prentice and a couple of Brion's watercolors were the only pictures on the exposed brick walls. A dull gray 'space heater' hung from the ceiling. The entire place was lit by overhead bulbs. In those days it was a score, but in the eerie quiet, it seemed a hardy proposition for a 60-year-old guy living alone.

... Audrey and the Dib continue on. The city is deserted. The air colder. Audrey is sick and spits up blood. "Lulow" crosses their path, a sure sign they are in a bad place. They check into the "Globe Hotel." A Japanese with phosphorescent facial scar tissue and a young black guy fix Audrey up with some "old style painless" ...

In daylight, Franklin Street was a very different story. During office hours, lower Manhattan was one of the most densely populated areas in the world. Several thousand people worked in the newly-built World Trade Center Towers alone.

... Illustrations for Crawdaddy! *magazine ... political potlatch ... interactive art galleries ... looking to Sirius ... Ah Pook sketches for Armageddon ...*

The money ran out in no time. I was flipping a coin sometimes to decide whether to buy milk for tea or a pack of cigarettes for the day. Inevitably, I had to look for freelance work. It was my first New York summer and the apartment had no air conditioner. It also had no table. When I finally picked up illustration assignments for *National Lampoon* and Marvel Comics, I had to paint with them resting on my knees.

Bill suggested I work at the loft whenever I needed, and gave me a key. He'd started a monthly column for *Crawdaddy!* magazine called "Time of the Assassins" and for a few months I also supplied illustrations for that.

I was at the loft one evening finishing up one of them when he came home from a dinner party. He'd had a few drinks, naturally. He came over and placed a piece of hash on the desk.

"Here! I got a present for you!"

"Well thanks, Bill. I'll smoke it later."

"No, man! It's not dope! It's aphrode-e-e-siac! Ted Morgan gave me a bunch of it. Got it down in South America. Says it really works."[27]

"Great! I'll save it for a special occasion."

We talked about the picture for a while then he wandered off.

Five minutes later I noticed it was very quiet. As I was packing up my stuff to leave I saw the back of his head on the other side of the kitchen counter. He still had his hat on. It wasn't moving. I figured he'd fallen asleep in the chair so I crept over to wake him.

When I came around the corner of the counter, I found him very much awake, sitting in his boxer shorts, staring intently down at his crotch.

"Not-a-fu-cking-twitch!" he said.

Another time when I stopped by, I found him busy at the stove.

Plastic shopping bags covered the kitchen counter. He'd read an article in *High Times* magazine proposing that opiates could be extracted from lettuce. *Lactuca virosa* — wild lettuce — does have such properties. Head lettuce from Chinatown does not. Nevertheless, Bill had decided to commit himself to an all-day vigil over a saucepan to prove things one way or the other — watching pounds of lettuce distil down to a black tar.

When I asked him later how it had turned out, he said that it had tasted like shit and it hadn't done shit. As always, he knew whereof he spoke.

It made sense that he would encounter the occasional dud. His quest for mind-altering chemicals covered a territory few, if any, have dared countenance. In the course of his life, he sampled just about everything in the pharmacy and washed it down with just about everything in the liquor store. That the endeavor resulted in one of the most far-reaching imaginations in literary history is testament to his methods. Given the fact that he would continue to create to the ripe old age of 83, his liver by rights should be in The Smithsonian.

... Audrey and the Dib continue on through a deserted New York City ... car wrecks litter the sand-covered streets and Lulow — a marsupial porcupine — crosses their path ... Audrey is sick ...they check into the Globe hotel and score some old-style painless from a Japanese pusher and his young black assistant ...

Along with his many forays into mind-altering chemistry, Bill also pursued mind-altering disciplines. From Scientology to Reich's Orgone theories, to Robert Monroe's astral cadets. (At age 60, he'd just signed on for out-of-body flying lessons when I arrived in New York.) With most of his interests, he appeared to apply an *à la carte* methodology. Taking what he felt relevant and disregarding the rest.

Many years later, a Scientologist ironically would perfectly characterize such a strategy. When asked if he was still "into it" he replied: *"Why not? It's like a supermarket, right? You don't have to buy everything."* Probably not a response that would bode well with the church elders, but certainly an attitude that worked for me.

I soon became familiar with Bill's New York friends. Apart from time at the loft, I also joined him for him for dinner parties and social events. Ted Morgan and his wife, Nancy, were hosts to several dinners. Ted was working on his biography *Literary Outlaw: The Life and Times of William S. Burroughs*. Nancy was researching a biography of Mary Shelley. Felicity Mason, aka Anne Cummings, was also finishing her novel, *The Love Habit*. Felicity was a former English debutante who'd helped Bill through one of his heroin withdrawals in London.

"I stood matches at the end of the bed for him to shoot at with his BB gun," she told me. She organized Sunday brunches for groups of 'art and literary' types.[28]

Naturally, Bill also had close gay friends, the most familiar being James, the new traveling companion I'd met in San Francisco. The *"We"* of his letter to me back then was now very apparent. He was clearly starting to take charge of Bill's affairs.

I'd known Bill for a while. He'd never struck me as a tough businessman. He was so self-effacing and preoccupied with work he didn't have the time or the wherewithal. He certainly wasn't forceful. In the entire time I knew him, I didn't hear him raise his voice once.

In his managerial role, James relieved Bill of that aspect of things and, consistent with his letter to me in San Francisco, now handled all Bill's communications to and fro. He answered Bill's mail, organized Bill's readings, edited Bill's texts, and answered Bill's phone. He was also invariably present whenever Bill and I spent time together.

Then there was Jacques — Jacques 'Loup' Stern de Rothschild, the craziest and most likeable of all Bill's friends. I met him on Franklin Street at the front door — then carried him up the stairs.

Jacques had contracted polio when he was 18 and spent most of his time in a wheelchair. He was remarkably knowledgeable over a wide range of subjects, particularly mathematics, and when topped up with Methedrine he could hold forth in a manner that was unassailable. Especially since he mixed fact and fiction quite freely. His mother had been a mistress of de Gaulle, whom he hated. Which is why he'd tried to kill him. The 'Loup' in his name, he said, was the basis for the film *The Jackal*. But he really had come close to a Nobel nomination for math.

His financial arrangements were vague. There were times when he clearly had a great deal of money and others when he clearly did not.

Sometimes he'd ask me to drive him around in the Cadillac, other times to meet him at the base of the Grand Central ramp, where he'd spent the day in his wheelchair trying to pull off a fake accident scam. Sometimes he seemed completely alone, other times he was being taken care of by extremely attractive young women.

He was authentic, eccentric, and completely unpredictable. He was also one of the sincerest advocates of my work. His screenplay *The Creation of Adam*, co-written with Bill, included descriptions of sets to be designed by me.

When he saw the Ah Pook artwork he offered to set me up in a loft and fund me to finish it. Based on that idea, I returned to San Francisco and picked up the remainder of my stuff. When I got back, there was no sign of Jacques and no sign of a loft. I would discover in time that this was simply his m.o. He'd resurface in time. In the meantime, I had a car full of just about everything I owned and nowhere to put it.

Painter friend Brian, who I'd met in the 'army,' had driven back with me and happened to have a friend of a friend's address in Brooklyn. Sharron, a true friend, let me stay at her place for nine months for free. She didn't have room for all my belongings, though, so I stored them with Bill's assistant, James, and his partner, Richard, in their place on the Bowery — a former YMCA locker room that would later become known as the Bunker. One late-night drop off there resulted in my first 'brush' with New York's finest.

It was 1:00 in the morning. Hardly anyone was around and I made a U-turn on Houston. When I pulled up in front of the building 50 yards down the street, a cop van pulled up right behind me. I didn't have my license or registration.

"I just popped over from Brooklyn," I told the flashlight.

"That's a big pop," came the answer.

They checked the glove compartment and rummaged around in the back. Then they had me open the trunk, by which time two beat cops had arrived. Everyone was pleased to see one another and was having a great old time regardless of me. One of them leaned in the driver's side and pointed at the half-dozen badges I had pinned to the roof upholstery.

"Where d'you get somethin' like that?" he asked.

It was a souvenir from *Swank* magazine — the first New York 'girlie magazine' I'd worked for — a large circular badge featuring a photograph of a 'girlie' pudendum.

"It was a present... you want it?"

"Yeah."

"Would that be considered a bribe?"

"Get outta here!"

I handed it to him and off they all went.

G-i-i-i-irls *are* good for some things it seems...

... *Armageddon ... St. Louis barracks to the 'End of the World'* ...

I discovered that January was the deadline for applications for CAPS (Creative Artists Public Service) Grants, so I stopped illustrating Bill's *Crawdaddy!* column and spent a solid three months working on the beginning of the final sequence in the book.

By December, it was two feet wide and over twenty-five feet long.

Making a copy was out of the question. On deadline day, I stuck the original in a wooden box, showed up at the 34th Street Post Office in Manhattan, attached the application and postage, and committed it to the void.

I did take a few 35mm slides of some of the details, and when Bill gave a reading from *Ah Pook* at NYU around that time, they were projected onto the wall behind him along with other images from the book. The combination of Bill's voice and giant pictures of the End of the World got a few good laughs from the audience.

One of the purposes of the event was to introduce his holiness, Chögyam Trungpa, to the student body. The Rinpoche had established The Naropa Institute as an adjunct to his Buddhist Center in Boulder, Colorado. By hiring prominent poets and writers, he hoped to attract a smarter, wealthier crowd of adherents. Allen Ginsberg and Anne Waldman had set up *The Jack Kerouac School of Disembodied Poetics* for that purpose and Bill had signed on as one of the prominent writers.

He introduced me to the Rinpoche at the reception on Howard Street after the reading.

His holiness remained seated, on account of injuries, I was informed, that he'd sustained while driving drunk through a joke and novelty store window. He put down his cigarette and extended his hand, keeping a firm grip on the pita bread sandwich chock full of meat with the other, and careful not to knock the tumbler of alcohol from the arm of the chair. His young English wife, standing to his right, deferentially stopped 'whispering' in his ear. He was a burly man, reminiscent, I thought, of an underworld boss from a Bruce Lee movie. Despite his contention that 'now' was all that mattered, he wore a particularly large wristwatch.

I asked Bill where the holiness fit in.

"The Rinpoche has many incarnations to reconcile in this lifetime," said Bill.

Allen Ginsberg also read at the NYU performance but I didn't meet him at the time. That also happened at the Franklin Street loft.

I'd been working on a deadline for a freelance job and showed up after dinner. Allen was cracking chicken bones and sucking the marrow — much of which was on his beard. Bill introduced us.

"You're cute. Do you fuck boys?" asked Allen without missing a suck.

"Now, now, Allen," said Bill.

"No," insisted Allen. *"He's cute. So do you?"*

Bill bailed me out.

"I have a riddle for you all," he announced. *"Yesterday, I got paid by* Crawdaddy *— in cash. Last night, before I went to bed, naturally I got a le-e-e-tle paranoid... so I hid it. This morning — wouldn't you know it? — I couldn't remember where the fuck I'd put it. Eventually I found it. My question is: where was it?"*

Allen, James, and the other two guests each had an answer, but I saw it clear as day between us.

"In the toaster," I said.

"Correct," said Bill.

"How d'ya do that?!" asked Allen.

"It was right there. It was bread, right? Where else would you put it?"

In the spring of '76 the lease was up on the Franklin street loft and Bill, weary of the walk up, decided not to renew it. He suggested I take it over.

It was customary for incoming loft tenants to pay the outgoing for any improvements they'd made. Given that many of these spaces were raw when they were first occupied, the 'fixture fees' could be quite substantial — in Bill's case, amounting to around $7,000. A sum almost equivalent to the entire advance for *Ah Pook* and for Bill, in those days, a big percentage of his yearly earnings. Nevertheless, he agreed to forego it in order for me to have the place. I'd known Bill for a while now — I thanked him and suggested we talk later to confirm the offer.

Early the next morning, I got a call from James.

"You should forget about the offer altogether," he said. *"William was tripping when he made it."*

An odd remark, considering Bill's aversion to LSD. He certainly hadn't looked like he was tripping. Maybe he meant Bill was just out of his mind; an even odder idea. I took it at face value and next time I saw Bill, I acknowledged there'd been a change of plan.

He was quite incredulous. *"What are you talking about, man? I gave it to you! It's* yours!*"*

If anyone was tripping, apparently it was James.

When I called him on it later, his response was remarkably candid:

"I admit I've gone out of my way to obstruct you on occasions," he said. *"I put it down to sibling rivalry."*

I moved in, in May of '76. Bob Gale, illustrator and collaborator on Bill's *Book of Breeething*, showed up soon after.

Bob is one of the most remarkable draftsmen I've ever known. He'd also met Bill in London but this was the first time we'd met one another.

"Never discuss a work in progress," was one of Bill's earlier admonitions and it certainly held true when it came to collaborations with artists. He'd worked with English artist and writer Jeff Nuttall on *My Own Mag* for some time before I'd met him but he didn't mention him or show me any of the work they'd produced together. Similarly, it was only by chance that I ran into Steve Lawson, another illustrator Bill had started working with, as Lawson was leaving Duke Street. True to his literary maxim, Bill declined to discuss the project they were working on. By the same token, Bob had never heard of me, either.

Bob was a poignant reminder of how far I'd come with *Ah Pook* and how far I still had to go. We had a lot of Bill Burroughs stories in common.

He'd also eaten at the notorious Angus Steak House with Bill, but unlike me he hadn't encountered the Old Man of the Mountain there. (That would be seven years later in Boulder, Colorado). One evening, both well lit, they'd left the Steak House and stopped into an amusement arcade in Piccadilly where Bill liked to work out on the shooting range. Even though he was *"extremely drunk,"* said Bob, Bill could fire a gun with *"terrifying"* accuracy.

Bob was working freelance for the *New York Times* and gave me a name to call. Political illustration didn't pay much but every bit counted. Over the course of the next couple of years, I worked for almost every section of the paper and got a firsthand look at the journalistic methods of one of America's foremost organs of dissemination.

Jacques resurfaced in '76 and was busy producing his movie — which had now become *Junky*. Bill and Terry Southern were rewriting it with assistance from Dennis Hopper, as Jacques wheeled around, handing out points and retainers left and right. I was hired as Art Director, Divine was to play "Lupita," Patti Smith "Mary," and Bob Dylan was supposedly to supply the music. Dennis would also direct and/or star as Bill. Joe Bianco, who became a good friend, acted as the legal intermediary between Jacques and everyone else.

A man on speed in a wheelchair is a difficult man to pin down.

Chaos was Jacques's particular art form, and this turned out to be one of his masterpieces. After umpteen rewrites and a round of over-the-top parties, the project finally collapsed under its own weight. The movie was over.

As Bill would say: *"It weren't great, but it was good copy."*

In September of that year, *Swank* magazine, whose 'beaver badge' had saved my ass on the Bowery, agreed to publish an excerpt of *Ah Pook* in their offshoot magazine, *Rush*. The pages, which appeared in December, were taken from the twenty-five foot end sequence.

After several months in the void, it had finally resurfaced. The artwork was intact but there was no note, no nothing. Certainly no grant money. These would be the only pages ever published and the last finished images I'd produce. Appropriately, there were 11 pages, the same as there had been when the project started. And consistent with its origins, it began in a *barracks*, a recruitment center for a very different kind of 'middle-sex' volunteers.

... an abandoned army barracks outside St. Louis MO, Audrey, The Dib, Cumhu, Xolotl, Ouab, Guy and Jimmy the Shrew are sleeping ... Old Sarge wakes them

and tells Cumhu and Xolotl to "Fuck out some weaponry." They protest that sexual intercourse between them is forbidden, but Old Sarge insists. ... a black egg is created from which a "Black Captain" emerges. A being who attacks the racial rage centers. "Mrs. Worldly" is a victim of this effect. Audrey Carson as a hotel desk clerk, responds to her imperious manner by turning into a Black Captain. She turns black with rage and explodes like a "ruptured sausage" ... Old Sarge then orders Audrey and Ouab to "...fuck out a red biologic." A self-replicating hermaphrodite which attacks the sexual rage centers. "Reddies" pop up at an America first rally, dissolving the outraged convention goers into "... steaming piles like boiled lobsters." ... In response, a horde of vigilantes sweeps up from the Bible belt ... "hanging every living thing in their path." They're intercepted by the Reddies and destroyed ... Virus B23 is dropped on the cities of the world. "Any sex act can now create life. The biologic bank is open" New species arise to replace the old human conditions forever. The "heroes of the fever" head for the last roundup: Hieronymus Bosch's **Garden of Earthly Delights** ...

Rush paid $1300 for the 11 pages. Bill let me keep most of it. It brought the total amount I'd had to work with in six years to around $5,000. I'd redesigned the book into a horizontal format to add to the feeling of a panorama. Seeing it crammed back into a vertical shape proved it had been the right decision. It didn't look good but it was an inevitable compromise. The title for the excerpt though wasn't:

Ah Pook is Here

by WILLIAM S. BURROUGHS

with full illustrations by Malcolm McNeil

I'd been reduced to "illustrator" — someone who comes along *after* a text is complete.

Continuing to support the project with freelance work in a city like New York was next to impossible, and the process of starting and stopping was becoming harder and harder to sustain. The only way to keep *Ah Pook* afloat was through the investment of another mainstream publisher. Our agent, Peter Matson, had explained the problems in finding one of those several times. The most obvious difficulty he said, was *"...simply getting the material around."*

We'd hoped that the published images in *Rush* might help solve that problem. In fact, they did the opposite, in that they explicitly demonstrated that a book full of such material would be a legal and therefore, a financial impossibility.

The unassembled nature of the artwork wasn't the real issue. Any publisher could see from looking at the dummy and a couple of finished frames what the book would look like. The real problem was content — more specifically the translation of word content into image.

"Words imply. A painting has to specify." It wasn't the Martian's *arm* that was in question.

As Peter put it euphemistically: *"... this project is too far out and/or expensive for the more conventional publishing houses."*

Meaning: the explicit nature of the artwork precludes any mainstream publishing investment whatsoever. Or: the very moment I'd started making pictures of Bill Burroughs's ideas, *Ah Pook* had been dead in the water. It ended at the beginning.

In keeping with the reciprocal nature of the process, I'd done exactly what Mr. Hart had told me to do: *"GO OUT AND GET THE PICTURES. AND ESPECIALLY THE ONES WE CAN'T PRINT."*

The book had demonstrated its basic contention: the Images of Sex and Death are tightly censored by the status quo in order to assert Control.

Job done. Q.E.D. after seven years of work.

Cheaply produced comics and magazines that feature this kind of material are tolerated because they're marginal publications. Similarly, the porno industry, being a fundamental part of the status quo, is allowed to publish so called 'explicit' material, but that environment is also tightly controlled.

Ah Pook fell into neither of these categories. It wasn't cheap to produce and the material was far too intellectual to pass as pornography. Porno and ideas are antithetical. 'Less plot, more twat' is axiomatic to the idiom.

Despite the reality being the *sine qua non* of all mammalian life, representations of penile erections *shall not* be found in any section of Barnes and Noble Booksellers. It's likely to be that way for a long time to come. It was only a few years earlier, that Bob Guccione had shocked America by revealing that women had pubic hair. *Penthouse* was a landmark publication, but in order to soften the blow, it still had to photograph the precious four square inches of turf, as Lenny Bruce put it, through a diffusing screen.

Hard on its heels came Richard Nixon's "war on pornography." The year we signed the contract with Straight Arrow, he declared that so long as he was *"... in the White House, there [would] be no relaxation of the national effort to control and eliminate smut from our national life."*

Nixon had a particular problem with gay folks. In San Francisco, he said, they were everywhere. Not just in *"... the ratty part of town,"* but in the *"upper class"* as well. It was *"... the most faggy goddamned thing you could ever imagine..."* So pervasive, in fact, that he wouldn't *"shake hands with anybody from San Francisco."*[29]

And as for The Comics Code Authority:

General Standards — Part C
COSTUME

1   Nudity in any form is prohibited, as is indecent or undue exposure.
2   Suggestive and salacious illustration or suggestive posture is unacceptable.
3   All characters shall be depicted in dress reasonably acceptable to society.
4   Females shall be drawn realistically without exaggeration of any physical qualities.

Women as human skin suits becomes a complicated issue within these restraints — even if their "physical qualities" *aren't* exaggerated. Quality is an impossible thing to illustrate anyway, although it could be argued that few things are as honest as an erection — it's one of the sincerest indications of feeling and intent. (At that time at least. Viagra would ultimately put paid to the idea) To complicate matters, the erections depicted in *Ah Pook* were mostly being passed around amongst guys — some of whom were part something else. A factor that goes beyond the pale as far as obscenity is concerned and one that further diminished the possibilities of mainstream investment.

Regardless of the censorship issues, at the time there simply wasn't a market for illustrated books of that nature. It would take George Lucas to establish that. After *Star Wars*, full-color illustrated fantasy and science fiction books and magazines became a billion dollar industry almost overnight. A market that increased commensurately with cheaper and cheaper means of reproduction.

But that was in 1977. By then I'd already quit.

Soon after the *Rush* publication, Nancy Morgan introduced me to the director of the *Marlborough Gallery*, Rome. I showed her the artwork and she agreed to an exhibition once it had been completed. Most significantly, she discussed the idea of a joint venture between two or three European publishers.

Europeans had been publishing long form comic books — *bandes dessinées* — for years, and many of them involved sexual content that was no less explicit than *Ah Pook*. I'd always considered it a market that had been ignored and, given the insurmountable difficulties in the US, it seemed like the only possibility left.

Agent Peter Matson however, didn't share my enthusiasm. He looked out the window of his office and said: *"That all sounds very complicated to me."*

With that remark, the book came to an end. There was nowhere left to go.

In retrospect, Peter was doing me a favor, but at the time I felt a level of disappointment and disorientation I'd not known before. The idea had been my frame of reference for a very long time. I'd followed it from one city to another, one country to another, trying to see it through. I'd finally found a means, I thought, for keeping it going. With a seemingly disinterested wave of the hand, it felt like all of that had been dismissed. In the end, that was all it took. With a single sentence, seven years of work went out the window.

I continued seeing Bill and continued providing images for other texts with him. *Ah Pook* might be over but rapport between words and images was still intact. Things would continue to *happen*. There were a lot more 'blurry' moments to come.

When Bill was moving out of Franklin Street, I'd asked him if I could have his rocking chair. Not because I needed furniture, but I'd often seen him sitting there rocking and thinking, and I'd like it as a keepsake. Generous as ever, he agreed. He also left behind an old freestanding wardrobe that I *hadn't* asked for.

His new place was 222 Bowery, the ground floor of the former Y.M.C.A. where James and Richard had lived. In keeping with its stark subterranean aspect, it had been officially named "The Bunker": a sound-proof, bulletproof, all-white concrete emplacement with a couple of small windows for air. Access was through a sequence of two locked gates and a heavy metal door. You phoned from the street to be let in.

One time when I stopped by, I asked Bill if he'd seen anything unusual while he was living on Franklin Street.

"Like what?" he asked.

"Smudges," I said. *"Sometimes I see black smudges out of the corner of my eye."*

"Whereabouts exactly?"

"By the door. Near the wardrobe."

"Hmmm... that would make sense," he said.

The idea didn't seem to surprise him at all but he didn't offer any more information.

When I got home, naturally I checked it out. I looked inside, under-neath, and pulled it away from the wall. Then I stood on a chair and looked on top.

There I discovered a small note in Bill's handwriting.

Two dried up lemon slices were alongside and it was sprinkled with salt. It was a curse, the 'Curse of the Blinding Worm' to be exact, one of the many he'd recited to me back in London. They'd been taught to him by his nanny when he was a child, he'd said. Beneath the note was a newspaper clipping — an unflattering review of *Exterminator!* by Anatole Broyard.

The image of Bill standing on a chair intoning his way through this ritual was priceless enough, but what was interesting was the manner in which it had been revealed to me. I *had* thought I'd seen smudges and Bill seemed to know all about them.

What smudges?

Anatole Broyard was *The New York Times* book critic for over a decade and Bill had fallen into the exalted company of the likes of James Baldwin and Christie Brown as a victim of his sometimes vitriolic reviewing style. Bill was no fan of book reviewers. Not just in terms of his own books but as an unacceptable idea in general. In Ted Morgan's biography, *Literary Outlaw: The Life and Times of William S. Burroughs,* published several years after I'd discovered the curse, Bill discussed them at length.

He compared them to the Egyptian 'Assayers of Scribes,' the court historians who enforced the interests of their employers and forestalled opposition. They were the arbiters of taste, the controllers of information, the ultimate censors. It was they who determined what would be read and who would read it. Bill wanted to *"... put a curse on all of them."* Referring obliquely to the reviewer in question, he pictured the effect of such a curse:

"This afternoon he has delivered his latest review to the office...a perfect demolition job and he knows it. The effect is disquieting, gathering to itself a legion of negation. A feeling that someone is at the door. He steps to the peephole, the hall is empty. He slides the deadbolt and opens the door. A small black dog slithers in without a sound, brushes past his leg as light as wind. When he tries to find the dog it is nowhere to be found."

Those smudges?

While I was researching this book, I went online to see what else I could find about Broyard.

Appropriately, he was a man whose life was shrouded in mystery. As a writer he was compromised by a personal dilemma — he refused to publicly acknowledge his 'black' heritage. Passing himself off as 'white,' he fought all his life to maintain a precarious illusion, a deceit that possibly frustrated his own attempts as a sincere novelist. The effect of which was a level of volatility that could sometimes express itself quite dramatically and quite forcefully.

On one occasion, according to editor Gordon Lish, when writer Burt Britton alluded to Broyard's 'black' ancestry, *"He snapped like a dog snapping. He barked at Britton."*[30]

Broyard was born in New Orleans. His name in all likelihood derives from the French 'brouillard' meaning fog. The verb 'brouiller' means to mix or muddle up, jam, confuse, or blur...

To *smudge*, as it were.

But if Bill had originated the curse, what were the smudges doing by *his* wardrobe?

He continues in *Literary Outlaw*:

"However, curses are tricky. They can bounce back, and they can bounce back double."

Cursing amounts to dialogue. Given Broyard's heritage, it's possible he *also* had a nanny. Events soon after I'd found the note seemed to suggest something of the sort.

I'd driven to New York for several reasons: Bill was there, there was more likelihood of other illustration work there and if I didn't like it, I would be halfway home. Friend Pete who'd sold me the car also had a cousin there whose father had been a prosecutor at Nuremburg. He might be able to help with a green card, thought Pete. Cousin John, it turned out, had a girlfriend named Valerie. A year later she moved in to Franklin Street. Two years later I married her. I never met the prosecutor. I did get my green card.

Not long after I'd discovered Bill's curse, I mentioned to Valerie that my last few illustration projects had all started out fine, but then at the very end I'd screwed them up. She decided a "negative influence" was at work and assured me she'd take care of it.

Her solution was a week-long ritual in which a foul-smelling rope of incense had to be burned each day. Since I'd complained about the smell and even left the loft on account of it, she took to burning it at night — in the bathroom. On the sixth night, the bathroom burst into flames. If not for the insomniac neighbor downstairs, the whole building would probably have caught fire.

What's *really* tricky about curses, it seems, is not that they might bounce back, but it might not be *you* they bounce back on. Having established the dialogue, one of the protagonists may physically move from the point of transmission — leaving the line still open. One party is still dialing the same number, unaware that the former subscriber is no longer there. When a third person inadvertently comes on the line, the results can be disastrous.

As a precaution — and a courtesy — therefore, cursing, like all potentially repercussive activity, should probably not be done from home.

It's better to use the corner payphone, as it were. Like a wise English bobby once told me:

"Don't keep the shit on the premises!"

Spells, incantations, and curses are a means by which words — and images — supposedly *effect* over distance — hence Bill's fascination with them. *"...[S]avoring the rich folk lure of spells and curses."*[31] as Mr. Hart would have it. His claim to have put a coffee shop in London out of business using such methods is documented in several biographies. The connection between intention, method, and result, however, is ultimately viewed as circumstantial. *Coincidental.* Such methods fail the first test of scientific rigor: controlled repeatability. They are not considered a dependable resource and are invariably dismissed outright.

Even so, the same systematic use of word and image might be said to characterize the manipulative processes of media — the primary method of Control: Selective, repetitious use of words and images with deliberate intention to *effect* a specific outcome. Millions of people infected (at a distance) with the same imagery, same values, and same sense of events behaving in a similar way.

"So long as the calendar of animated cartoons implanted in the minds of the workers continues to operate, the control system can predict future behavior with the same accuracy as it can reconstruct past behavior."[32]

Bill had proposed this idea in the context of the Maya, but television 'programming,' with its relentless, 24-hour-a-day barrage of 'curses and incantations' dulls and controls critical thought and directs fostered anxiety and aggression according to specific agendas. A technological 'blinding worm' that never sleeps. Again:

"Don't keep the shit on the premises!"

"Los Ninos Locos" ... National Screw *magazine ... wild boys are released in the butterflies of fear...*

As a footnote to incendiary moments around Bill, Steve Lawson, the third English illustrator that he'd recruited in London, visited New York around that time. Bill was out of town, so Steve had stayed at the Bunker. He called me the morning after he got there to tell me he'd hardly slept all night and needed my help. The neighbors had pounded on the door around 2:00 a.m. and he'd woken up to find the bed all around him on fire.

Being his first time in New York, he had no idea where to buy a new mattress, much less dispose of the remains of the old one. He also had to repaint the bedroom wall. He figured he must have 'fallen' asleep with a cigarette in his mouth.

Similarly, when Bob Gale first arrived in New York he, too, stayed at the Bunker. While he was there, the building next door caught fire.

Smudges in air: a convoluted "coincidental" method for communicating ideas but *effective* nevertheless.[33] As a conceivable boost to transmission, one of the images I was working on at the time was for Bill's *Day is Done*...

... Militant 'dykes' attempt to destroy an enclave of Wild boys ... The Wild boys retaliate in the form of phantom dogs ...

Coincidence had initiated *Ah Pook* and the fact that they kept occurring had helped sustain it. They were an affirmation of sorts, a sense of being in the right place at the right time.

Coincidences force us to pause momentarily and *look*. They are moments of being *Here*. Like signposts in our inner landscape they *orient* us telling us where we are and suggesting a possible course of action — either literal or figurative. In a very real sense we are presented with a moment of *giving way*. As with any signpost we can choose to acknowledge them or ignore them. Given the number that occurred during *Ah Pook* I couldn't help but acknowledge them.

I also considered the possibility of trying to *force* them to occur.

The old joke runs that men bought magazines like *Playboy* for the articles, but the fact is, 'girlie magazines' like *National Screw* and *Swank* did print a lot of fiction. Along with Marvel Comics, *National Lampoon,* and *The New York Times,* they became my primary source of illustration work. One of them was *Gallery* magazine and, after a couple of assignments, editor Joe Spieler suggested I write and illustrate my own monthly series.

I came up with *Tetra*. In the pitch I wrote:

"... there are three ways of seeing: I see things as they are in reality with my conscious vision. I see things in my dreams with my subconscious vision and I see things with my imagination. But there is a fourth way that sees beyond time and space. That sees people at a distance. Even those that are dead. That hears people talking when they're not there. That sees the future..."

This fourth way I imagined might be contingent on a particular alignment of the other three. I would assign characters to each and make them operate within their own contexts. One would be purely imaginative, one would be a record of my dreams, and the third would be me living in everyday New York City. By making the three interact with one another, I might achieve an alignment. A coincidence. Why not?[34]

A pin-up magazine was an unlikely place for such an idea but Joe managed to convince the owners. It had one thing going for it: the protagonist was a woman.[35] After seven years, I could finally shake my head loose of mutant boys.

The project was relentless — five pages a month in full color. Like *Ah Pook*, the images weren't 'comic' and this time I had to come up with the words as well. Many times I would be sitting in the *Gallery* offices on deadline day, desperately trying to finish a page while the art director paced up and down waiting to paste it in. The moment I finished one episode, I had to get right on to the next.

I stuck with it for almost two years and was about to introduce the 'dream' character, when I finally *had* to quit. I was handed *another* full time job and the two schedules weren't compatible. In December '79, I became a father. It wasn't the alignment I'd had in mind, but I'd ended up with an effect that, in a sense, *did* show me the future.

Orien was born on Pearl Harbor day at exactly 8:00 a.m., and, being six weeks premature — a sneak attack. He was just over two pounds when he arrived. When I took him over to the Bunker to introduce him to Bill, he was up around four pounds.

It was the end of the afternoon and Bill was seated at the big conference table with his first glass of vodka in front of him. James was standing alongside.

"*So Ma-a-a-alcolm. Does the child have a godfather?*"

"*No Bill, are you offering?*"

"*It would be a pleasure! Bring the child to me!*"

I passed him off and Bill settled him on his left knee, holding him with his left hand. He reached for the vodka with his right and took a healthy swig. He swallowed, carefully put down the glass, then rubbed his hand around and around on top of Orien's head.

"*I now pronounce you my Go-o-o-odchild!*" he intoned.

The Pope had nothing on that.

Despite the workload on *Tetra*, I was still able to honor one last commitment to *Ah Pook*.

Back in 1977, Bill and I had decided to publish the book in text form only, in the hope of attracting a publisher for the full version. Bill would write an introductory preface recounting the project's history and, naturally, we agreed I'd create the cover.

I produced an abridged version of the one I'd originally intended: a Mayan wall relief showing the confrontation between Ah Pook and the

American astronaut on the moon. I also supplied a 'hieroglyphic' version of the same scene to be used as endpapers. I brought them over to the Bunker for Bill's approval then handed them to James, who was in charge of the business arrangements.

The book would be published by Calder in 1979 under the title *Ah Pook is Here and Other Texts* but it would be a while before I could actually see it. Since it was only available in England, I'd asked my father to pick me up a copy. When he called to confirm where to send it, he mentioned that he'd read a couple of sections. Which sections, he didn't say. He was tempted to burn it, he said. Not exactly a good quote for the back of the book — especially with book burning being fundamental to the idea.

As it happened, for very different reasons, I would have a similar reaction.

The name had been officially changed to *Pook*. My cover hadn't been used at all. The endpapers were printed backwards and not credited. On the back cover, *Ah Pook is Here* was described as the "...new novel from William Burroughs." No mention was made of its beginnings or the fact that the text represented only half of the book.

I flipped through it to remind myself which parts might have upset my father and discovered that a series of sex scenes had been tacked on to the very end — male-to-male sex, obviously.

I'd used ejaculated birds, bats, and other flying creatures as a *graphic* transitional device in the sequence after Virus B23, but now they were presented literally. Young guys actually ejaculating goldfish, cherries, and so on. And now there were bat boys with flutes up their asses, Audrey with a rubber steering wheel up his ass, and boys on hang gliders powered by "nitrous farts."

All the old human conditions had been destroyed forever, but the 'treehouse' had apparently remained intact. It wasn't disturbing anymore, just depressing.

No real explanation was given for not using my cover. James's vague response was that it simply hadn't worked. Thirty years in the future, a dead man would lead to me to the real answer, right now I was sufficiently depressed not to care.

"Writing is a timely business," said Bill.

Ah Pook's time, it seemed, was up. I was done with it.

The expression 'body of work' was never more apt. In the end, I did what you do with most bodies — I 'buried' it. I stuck everything in the drawer of a flat file and did my best to forget about it.

Ah Pook was definitely not Here

Coincidentally, a wave of Iranian good stuff hit New York around that time and Bill went back onto heroin. He wasn't really here, either.

In the wake of that, he became the adopted figurehead for the New York 'downtown' music scene.[36] His celebrity image began to grow. The heavy hitters of rock now appeared in photographs alongside him.

In 1981, he made his network television debut on *Saturday Night Live*, introducing Dr. Benway to the world at large. He chose the shipwreck routine in which the good doctor commandeers a lifeboat dressed as a woman.

He also took a more hands-on interest in UFOs and the possibility of alien visitations.

Inspired by Whitley Streiber's book, *Communion*, he'd contacted the author and arranged a trip to his home in upstate New York. Streiber claimed several encounters had occurred there, but, much to Bill's chagrin, the aliens failed to appear on his behalf. Given their apparent preoccupation with rectal probes and Bill's remark about having seen God in his asshole, it seems they might have had a lot to talk about.

Then Billy Junior. The end of a *"short, unhappy life,"* at age 33.[37] Regardless of the liver transplant, he'd continued to drink heavily and eventually even stopped taking the anti-rejection medication. In an *Esquire* article prior to his death, he blamed his father for "ruining" his life.

It was a watershed year.

Cities Of The Red Night also appeared at that time, a book Bill must have been working on right after *Ah Pook*. In keeping with his ongoing narrative m.o., he'd picked up where he'd left off.

In the final scene of *Ah Pook*, the young heroes of the fever had boarded the *Marie Celeste* and sailed off into the sunset. Now began the record of their journeys.

Trusty Clem Snide represented Bill's primary voice this time around — a private detective searching first for a missing boy, then missing books, then the "producer" who would hire him to *write* those books and become the instrument of the narrative of which he himself was part.

Clem had an assistant now, a young artist able to draw an "identikit" image of the producer ahead of time, and work *with* his boss to create the accompanying images.[38] *"You will finish the scenario,"* insisted the producer. *"Your assistant will do the illustrations."*

Bill's description of the methodology was the same as the one I'd used for Ah Pook.[39] It was encouraging to see that such an arrangement had impressed itself sufficiently for him to use it as a literary device. It was less gratifying to see that the artist assistant was named James.

The book read like a manual. A relentless catalogue of spurting cocks, hangings, diseases, and weaponry so flat and humorless at times that the ship felt to be plowing through molasses. True to form, *"nothing was true"* but *"everything was permitted"* — everything that, is except women. If they appeared on deck at all, it was as whores, bitches, or anonymous breeders. It was a bleak, joyless voyage. Slowly, inexorably, *Ah Pook* slipped that much further over the horizon.

As did Bill himself.

At the end of the year, he decided to quit the Bunker and leave New York altogether. James moved back to Kansas and Bill went with him.

Then the Christmas cards stopped. No more wonderfully incongruous pictures of Santa in his sleigh, or reindeers and elves in the snow signed *"all the best, Bill."* The interaction, it seemed, had officially come to an end.

The documentary *Burroughs* was being filmed during this time and was finally released in 1983.[40] I saw it at the Bleeker Street Cinema when it opened.

There were no real surprises. Allen Ginsberg, John Giorno, Terry Southern, and the usual gang of suspects put in appearances. Bill's life story I was already aware of. Watching all the familiar scenes unfold was a strange sensation — the feeling of being part of something but no longer part of it.

James featured prominently in the film and on several occasions discussed his pivotal role in Bill's life. Often with the camera to himself, he confirmed how he'd now taken charge of all Bill's business affairs. With the same improbable candor, he also launched into his sibling routine again, this time with respect to Billy Junior:

"...see, I always felt funny dealing with Billy. I loved Billy, and — uh — felt like a brother to him. But you know how it is between brothers. There's a little rivalry.

"... I felt like he [Billy Jr.] looked at me as a reproach. A living reproach that I was the son that William wanted and not he."

It's unlikely Billy perceived of James in these terms anymore than I did. The fact that James was forthright enough to express it on camera, however, was consistent with his manner in revealing it to me and a clear indication of his determination to become *the* significant authority in Bill's world.

Most poignant were the images of Billy himself. The feeling of abandonment and alienation from his father were almost palpable. Contrary to James's competitive assertions,[41] Billy *was* a writer and a good writer. Writing is a timely business. Billy just never got enough of it. He would die during the course of the making of the film.

It was a depressing movie, a vindication of sorts, but hardly of any consequence now. In contrast to these intellectual father/son aspirations, I was now raising a real son in New York City — a process that determined a very different kind of perspective, one that, to me, eclipsed all other forms of observation.

Under the circumstances, Kansas was hardly a priority. The experience of *Ah Pook is Here* became so remote it was as if it had never happened.

I'd quit illustration by now and moved into sculpture, model-making, and set building.

Around 3:00 one morning, while I was working on a deadline in Brooklyn, I got a call from a video production company needing a *coffin* built — in *four hours*. I told the guy I was busy and suggested he rent one. Since I had him on the phone though, I set up an appointment to show my portfolio.

The company was Charlex and over the next couple of years I supplied them with models and sets for more than 70 projects. The owners had told me they were about to buy something called a Paintbox, an 'electronic paint system' that allowed you to airbrush onto video. It would be the first one in the country, they said. I would one of the first ones on it.

Paintbox was the device that truly defined the moment when video emerged from television as a distinct art form. Television could now be *designed* in a very different way. It was a surface for painting upon and animating.

Choreographing visual narrative ideas as *storyboards* was an easy transition and having precise 'blueprints' to work from made the process far more efficient. I was hired full-time as the company's designer and "The Charlex Look" became an industry standard.

Our signature animation technique was called "Frame Push," an idea I'd come up with based on the same concept as *Ah Pook:* a single continuous image. By 'stitching' frames of video together and moving them electronically left or right, it gave the illusion of a camera pan. The storyboards for these projects were long single images that, like a codex, could be viewed holistically or as separate scenes.

The first was eight feet long and the award-winning video that resulted would attract the attention of the producers of *Saturday Night Live.* I was asked to come up with something similar for their opening credits.

As chance would have it, my network debut would be on the same show as Bill. A panoramic image style based on a beat-up little Mayan book we'd looked at together in The British Museum would win me an Emmy.[42]

The new technology also enabled me to continue with the black-and-white and color and time-jumping routines from *Ah Pook.* I designed projects for the first time in which actors were electronically cut from past archival film footage and inserted into the present.

I saw the medium as a new art form, but advertising agencies quickly caught on to the 'look.' As the '80s wore on, I was designing and directing, and in many instances, *inventing* commercials. An idea completely antithetical to everything I thought Bill Burroughs stood for.

Kansas somehow moved even further away.

Bill considered Nixon to have been good for America. His impeachment had *"struck a blow to the whole diseased concept of the revered image"* and had given back *"the American virtue of irreverence and skepticism."*[43]

By the end of the decade however, the revered image was assuming even greater proportions and skepticism was sliding toward despair.

In 1980, as a prelude to the Reagan decade, John Lennon — one of the few remaining voices of reasonable protest able to organize demonstrations on a large scale — was assassinated. He was making a comeback after retiring briefly as a new father. In light of the God-fearing years to come, more *"Imagine there's no heaven"* and *"Nothing to kill or die for"* was not what America needed its citizens to hear.

With Reagan came Nicaragua and Iran-Contra. Massive drug imports, South American death squads, the invasion of Grenada, and the bombing of Libya. It was business as usual. Might was right. Greed was good. A new life form was spawned — the yuppie.

The swami tide had subsided by this time. Many of the originals had now embraced the American way, become celebrities, had fun with the local girls, bought fancy cars and houses, had run-ins with the law, settled down, or just moved on.

Whether or not Chögyam Trungpa reconciled any of his many life-times, only his holiness — or highness, as he later became — will ever know. His eccentric interpretation of Buddhist teaching came to a grinding halt when alcohol finally showed him the door at age 48. A decade of *"Crazy Wisdom,"* interspersed with drunken outbursts and sexual assaults on devotees, had had its day.

Two years later, he'd be back for another round, supposedly in the reincarnated form of Chokyi Senge, 12th Trungpa Tulku, aka "The Lion of Dharma" — a young man 'in the Now' who would *also* be seen sporting an enormous wristwatch.

Such methods for finding inner calm were apparently no longer so fashionable. Fundamental angst and the sense of despair was now becoming the province of a more insidious form of indoctrination. Unlike the kind of drug use that sought to *derail* the conditioned response, newer concoctions were being used to *enforce* it. In the years to come, psychiatry cop priests in cahoots with big business would out-push all the illicit drug dealers combined. For many, being addicted would now constitute 'normal.' The worst drug scourge in history would co-opt and Control the lives of millions.

In 1985, Bill's *Adding Machine* was published. Mr. Hart reappeared briefly in a chapter on personal Immortality:

"A tiresome concept...predicated on the illusion of some unchangeable precious essence, that is greedy old MEEEEEE forever."

Hart was a *"trillionaire"* by now and getting on in years. Understandably, he was busying himself with locating and transplanting his ego into a younger body. As Bill pointed out in his own inimitable way, though, there *is* no singular 'me' to be found, much less stuck someplace else.

He talked about Coincidence, contact with the dead, and, in a chapter on Control, revisited the idea using the analogy of a lifeboat at sea. In a chapter titled *"Les Voleurs,"* he also talked about our working methods on *Ah Pook.*

The book was a small collection of critical essays that provided an all-too-rare glimpse of his creative worldview. The acutely perceptive, hilariously insightful side of Bill that people who spent time with him came to know that was not so overtly stated in his fiction. 'Philosopher Bill,' in the tradition of Rabelais, Voltaire, Cervantes, and Swift, riffing on the absurdity of it all.

This was the side of Bill that had made the indelible impression on me.

Then there was the other side.

The Place of Dead Roads had also been published — the relentless catalogue of spurting cocks, pimply-faced boys, drugs, and weaponry continued. Bill's emphasis had apparently switched from dying to killing — and the ways of killing and descriptions of the effects went on. Sounds, smells, animals, diseases, words, feelings — just about anything could be used as a weapon to destroy the enemy.

What enemy?

And women?

Women should still *"... be regarded as the principal reservoir for the alien parasite."*

It felt like Bill was comfortably ensconced in the 'treehouse.'

Virus B23 also manifested in the 1980s in the form of AIDS. Cumhu's vision of the future had finally caught up with itself. The orgy scene around the statue of Eros, which had degenerated into a spectacle of disease now became reality. Over the next 25 years it would claim more than 20 million lives worldwide — with no cure in sight.

In the movies, Arthur C. Clarke's *"... promise and wonder of space"* of *2001: A Space Odyssey* was reduced to an area about the size of Texas in which Americans would simply blow stuff up in the name of good-versus-evil — and merchandising. 'Stars' and 'wars' became inextricably locked. Contrary to Bill's hopes, from now on *only* science and the military would go into outer space — real or imagined. In *2001,* commander Bowman had *drawn pictures* in his downtime aboard ship. In the relentless battle against evil, there could be no downtime.

Finally, in 1987, *The Western Lands* appeared, the last novel Bill would write. The quintessential Bill Burroughs, the Burroughs that had inspired me, the Burroughs that confirmed to me his place as one of the great literary minds of all time. Sentence after sentence of impeccable craft plowing through a mindscape no other writer has ever envisioned. Continuing on through the ambiguous no man's land between life and death to confront the fundamental angst that besets us all.

Bill revealed the scope of that territory with a range of apprehensions that to me surpassed all those who had preceded him in the endeavor — the journey into the face of one's own mortality. Image, sound, taste, smell, feeling, and intuition — and above all, the unique Burroughs humor that had rarely made it on deck in the two novels that preceded it.

The Western Lands were the reality of *here* — a here Bill described over and over as a sinking ship.

In his 70s now, he continued to explore other art forms. Hal Willner, among others, began producing audio recordings of his readings. He teamed up with mainstream musicians, including Bill Laswell on *Seven Souls* and *Hallucination Engine*. David Cronenberg attempted to bring him to a wider audience with his feature film version of *Naked Lunch*.

Inevitably, inexorably, Bill became more and more the 'revered image' himself. He made cameo appearances in movies, and finally — wouldn't you know it? — in commercials.

Then he started painting.

I moved to Prince Street in 1986 — right behind where the Bunker used to be. In 1991, I was invited to give a talk about my work at the Broadcast Design Awards in Seattle. I was introduced as *"...the man probably responsible for the most imitated [television] design style of the 1980s."* Ah Pook had paid off. In 1996, I traveled to Los Angeles to direct my first campaign for Dodge.

I'd directed in L.A. a few times but this was a three-month production. It was school vacation, so Orien came with me.

He was 16 now and, like a lot of his friends, was a fan of Bill and his work. Naturally, I'd told him about the godfather ceremony in the Bunker. It was a nice story but understandably not very substantial.

The computer animation and compositing for my job was being done at Digital Domain, the Santa Monica film production company started and owned by director James Cameron. He was now in the final stages of

Titanic and my project was one of several infusing money to help keep the project afloat. A skull-and-crossbones pirate flag flew over the complex of buildings where I would spend the next two-and-a-half months. An "auspicious" image:

Ah Pook was here.

During the project, I was given a tour of one of the *Titanic* insert stages and saw some of the models used in the production. As a former model maker and miniature set builder, I could appreciated the remarkable craftsmanship that had gone into the process. I also happened to have a particular fascination with *Titanic*.

When *Ah Pook* first started and I was searching for reference, I'd discovered magazines and newspaper clippings from the time of the actual event. They were full of images of dead folks — perfect for *Ah Pook* — so I'd bought them. These were also folks who'd *drowned,* which held a personal fascination and horror. In all the times I'd traveled back and forth to England, I'd been superstitious enough never to bring the magazines across the Atlantic with me.

Special effects editing is a long, drawn-out process with a lot of time spent waiting for paint to dry. The art director on my job was checking the newspaper one afternoon, trying to find something to do for a couple of hours, when he happened to notice there was an exhibition of paintings in Santa Monica — by William Burroughs

"You know Burroughs, right?"

I happened to have Bill's number in Kansas with me and called to see if he might be there. Someone happened to answer the phone and gave me James's cellphone number. James told me that they were indeed at the gallery, but would be leaving for the airport in two hours.

The string of coincidences had a familiar ring to them. Orien being in L.A. with me was one of them. He might have a chance to finally meet one of his all-time heroes. Someone who, when it really came down to it, was the reason he was *here* at all.

Track 16 and the *Robert Berman Gallery* had staged a combination retrospective of Bill's paintings titled *Concrete and Buckshot*. Dennis Hopper and Allen Ginsberg were amongst the crowd.

Bill was standing facing us in the foyer as we entered, James alongside. He was quite frail now and surprised and happy to see me. I introduced him to Orien and we moved to a large conference table to talk. James remained standing between Bill and I.

We talked for some time, oblivious to the people milling around taking pictures. I explained why Orien and I were in L.A., and how he, too, had become an admirer of Bill's work, something that had been inevitable, hardly on account of any prompting on my part. Then, terrified that he'd say 'no,' I asked him if he remembered the time he'd volunteered himself as Orien's godfather.

"Well of course!" he said. *"Bring me a catalogue!"*

He inscribed it:

"For Orien my Godson — William S. Burroughs July 17 1996"

In that moment, I was sitting at another table, far away. It was in London, in the middle of the afternoon and I was sitting across from a stranger. I was there because I'd drawn a picture — a single image that contained within it everything that would lead to here. Now he'd signed it.

The effect he'd had on me as an artist cannot be measured. The practical effects, however, can. The most significant of these had now joined us at the table. For me, the circle was complete.

I wouldn't see him again.

Bill Burroughs died August 2nd 1997. A heart attack followed several years of health problems. He was 83.

His funeral service was held August 6th, the anniversary of the day they dropped the bomb on Hiroshima — the initiating event in *Ah Pook is Here*. He'd lived in Lawrence, Kansas for the previous 16 years and those who'd come to know and care for him took the opportunity to confirm that fact publicly and say goodbye in their own way.

What followed was a series of rituals, each geared to the perceptions of afterlife, according to the various people involved.

Death had been the subject of *Ah Pook is Here*, so the manner of Bill's own, naturally, held a personal significance. It not only represented a poignant moment in the history of a friendship but also what I considered to be a significant chapter in the process of interaction that had defined it. In that regard, I couldn't help but acknowledge the contrasts between what I'd learned through working with him and the events that defined his passing.

It began as a traditional funeral with Bill embalmed and arranged in an open casket. The service took place at the Liberty Hall in Lawrence with Bill's "favorite" music being played and including the song *"For All The Saints Who From Their Labours Rest"* sung live by James Grauerholz's mother, Selda. Patti Smith and Oliver Ray recited poems.

The last entry in his diaries was used as the quote for the occasion:

"Love? What is it? Most natural pain killer what there is. LOVE"

Being Bill, the convention of jacket and tie in preparation for 'meeting the maker' seemed hardly out of character. Nevertheless, even though friends still subscribed to the idea that one had to 'look smart' for the occasion, they'd opted for a less formal look for him. James, Ira Silverberg, and John Giorno had decided on the wardrobe. As Giorno put it:

"We picked the things to go into William's coffin and grave, accompanying him on his journey in the underworld."

They'd sent him off in a dark green jacket (*"the best of his shabby clothes"*), blue jeans (*"the only ones clean"*), white shirt (*"his best"*), brocaded Moroccan vest, blue necktie, black shoes, and, of course, one of his trusty fedoras.

To this they'd added a collection of personal artifacts indicative of Bill's earthly endeavors. His French *Commandeur des Arts et Lettres* and American Academy of Arts and Letters pins were attached to his lapel. At Giorno's insistence, he was armed with his sword cane and his favorite snub nose .38 revolver.

"This [was] very important!" said John.

His eyeglasses, a ballpoint pen, and a joint were placed in his top pocket, along with some heroin. A copy of an album Giorno and Bill had recorded together was placed beside him. Finally, as an indication of his sexual preferences, presumably, a red bandana was placed in his back pocket. Appropriate accouterments, one might think, for a journey through *The Western Lands*.

A somewhat confusing get-up, on the other hand, for someone leaving from the *Bible Air* departure lounge.

Bill would ultimately be laid to rest in the family plot in St Louis, Missouri, a Christian arrangement in which attachment to earthly possessions is considered not only irrelevant but frowned upon, particularly a loaded .38 revolver. To further confuse matters, a Buddhist ceremony would then be held later, in which friends would attempt to re-route Bill through Nirvana.

John Giorno had already meditated over the body, *"doing Tibetan Nyingma Budhhist mediation practices,"* immediately following Bill's death. Forty-nine days later, in accordance with *Tibetan Book of the Dead* rules, a bardo event was held in Lawrence in the hope of easing Bill through possible further incarnations. A *"...twelve-foot mound of firewood, photographs, wadded newspaper kindling, book jackets, fireworks, shot-up targets, record and CD liner notes"* was ignited for the purpose.

Mixing and matching spiritual conviction in this way suggests an *à la carte*, more discriminating view of religion. The use of specific ritual however, contradicts that idea. It succumbs to the same superstition — the same great fear con laid down by organized religions from the get-go. The system of Control and spiritual undermining Bill had condemned throughout his career. As he pointed out in *Ah Pook*, there are no rules, no procedures, no correct *words*, for reliably dealing with *this* life, let alone the next.

In his writing and interviews he'd further consistently distanced himself from his family heritage. To be buried alongside them also seemed somewhat incongruous. During the time I worked with him, on a book entirely concerned with death, he never once proposed getting shot through with embalming fluids and being buried in a Christian graveyard — *"...buried under slag heaps of dead dogma, sniveling prayers and empty promises,"* that is.[44]

In a conversation with biographer Ted Morgan, he'd stated that he wanted to be cremated in Tangier and have his ashes dropped into the straits from Cape Spartel.[45] A simple, elegant and seemingly appropriate finale. No rituals needed, no dress code required. What happened to that idea? An idea so much more ironic in the context of Lawrence, Kansas, whose city motto is *"From Ashes to Immortality."*

The reference to "love" in his diaries was presented almost as the summarizing statement of his career. As if the man who had once said that *"Love is a con"* had realized the error of his ways and atoned. Many times 'love' *is* a con. This particular use of it appeared to be one of them. Continuing in this sentimental vein, the cover of the memorial program showed him looking out over a bed of red roses above the caption:

"Old man of letters embalmed in cats and roses."[46]

One of the many great portraits would have encapsulated the spirit of his life more simply and more elegantly, yet here instead was a deliberately contrived statement. Where was Benway in all this? AJ and his baboon? Kiki with his cock flipping out?

Sentimentality is the epitome of falsehood. It's in contradiction to everything Bill Burroughs stood for. He might have been 'off' on occasions, or over the top or in your face but he was never false. Dr. Benway slipping in guts spilled from the operating table reveals Bill's humanity in far more elegant terms than the Hallmark Card sensibility presented here. It leaves us with a view that belies and diminishes *the broad general view of things,* the perspective that truly characterized his worldview. Sentimentality has no place in that world. Sentimentality and the sickly optimism it implies is a way of sidestepping the issue. A means for not owning up. Of not being *Here.* It's the refusal to acknowledge *"...what's on the end of the fork"* — and live with the inevitable conclusions.

It was Bill Burroughs's ability to sustain such a vision without compromise that *drew* me into his worldview and sustained *Ah Pook is Here* for as long as it did. His death closed a chapter on a unique friendship and it was indeed poignant. Recording that event was inevitable and my observations inevitably were based on what that friendship — and *Ah Pook* — had taught me. It was worthy of note, but, in the end, it was what it was: an observation, and, as with all observation, mostly questions.

When it came down to it, Bill Burroughs had been crossing borders all his life. It seemed unlikely he would have problems crossing the big one — no matter what he had in his pockets. As it happened, maybe that ballpoint pen did come in handy.

Six years later he would send me a postcard.

AH POOK 2

"Like this! Death walks out into the field and kills the young corn god. Young corn god becomes a death seed from which another corn god will grow — birth and death in all its rich variety of an old outhouse."

— AH POOK IS HERE

LOS ANGELES

I moved to L.A. in the fall of '99. There was nothing much on the radio. The end was nigh. In a couple of months, the world was scheduled for collapse — brought down by a bunch of zeroes. Y2K: End of Days.

There's always a panic when the calendar rolls up zeroes, and this time there would be three. The millennium bug was predicted to crash the internet, satellite communications, bank records, missile launch codes, and just about everything else in the digital planetary infrastructure.

I'd found a house across from Dodger Stadium, a few hundred yards from the Los Angeles Police Academy. This would presumably be the last baseball season — ever. The cops, though, might persevere. They had tanks and helicopter gunships now.

I quit directing at the end of that year and went back to visual narratives of my own. The year after that came 9/11 and the beginning of the end of *Ah Pook is Here* — hooded vigilantes running through the woods, terrorists in planes, weapons of disease, the end of the world...

"A time in the future when law and order breaks down," I'd told the FBI guy when he'd asked about the picture.

"Frightening," he'd said.

Every culture has its aesthetic: its style of architecture, its clothes, its art, its music, even its military. It has its own *aesthetic of violence.* 9/11 was *Hollywood.* Frightening indeed. Hart's Control machine was working full throttle.

In 2003, the 'Dodge grant,' as I called it, started to run out so I asked friend Doug Apatow if he had any ideas for making money. Doug represented film designers. I had my director's reel, a couple of screenplays and design portfolio and hoped he could maybe help get me work in the film business. Instead, out of the blue, he suggested *Ah Pook.*

"How about a show of the artwork?" he said. *"That might be worth a few bucks."*

It wasn't such a good idea. As far as I was concerned, Bill had gone and *Ah Pook* had gone with him. Dragging all that up again was the last thing I needed. The fact that the idea had occurred so unexpectedly, though, gave me pause for thought. If there was one thing I'd learned from working with Bill it was that there's no such thing as a *chance* remark — especially if it involved *Ah Pook*.

"Izzy the Push," as Bill called him, is Ah Pook's right hand man.[47] No matter how unlikely the prompt, it was usually a good idea to follow it through. Despite misgivings, I decided to sort out the artwork to see if a show was feasible.

Just as I'd anticipated, I was 'back' in New York in no time, and feeling very depressed. That's what images do — they take you back.

Just like holiday snaps taken of an *external* trip, they're the record of an *internal* landscape that recalls the experience of being there. Unlike a photograph, however, which is captured within a fraction of a second, a created image can take months. Months of focused attention on a single idea. The result is in an intense *emotional glyph*. A time capsule, both in the sense of encapsulating a moment and the means for taking you to it. All the sensations that occur during its making are embedded within it. The people, the conversations, the feelings, even the weather at the time.

Above all, the feelings.

I continued sorting through them nevertheless and several things became apparent, the most obvious being that some of them were starting to fall apart. Colors had faded, patches had come unglued, and one or two had even been eaten by something or other. Left alone, they would probably just deteriorate altogether. Regardless of a show, given what they represented, it seemed unconscionable that there might be no record of them. On a practical level, even if I did decide to exhibit the artwork, in order to show what was available I would have to put together some kind of proposal. For both reasons, I decided to digitize it all.

It took a while, but I catalogued everything, including notes, letters, photos, and the original working text.

While I was at it, I decided to assemble some of the pages the way I'd envisioned them. It hadn't been possible back when they were created so this was the first time I was really able to see them. It was also the first time I could get a sense of how much work *had* been done. For a moment, I actually felt good about *Ah Pook*. I put together a dozen bound folders of images and explanatory copy and went looking for a gallery.

Track 16 had been the last place I'd seen Bill and through a mutual friend I'd since met the gallery manager, Laurie Steelink. Laurie liked the work and set up a meeting with owner Tom Patchett. Tom was also impressed, but before he could commit himself one way or the other, he felt I needed to write about it. Explain what it was and where it had been all this time. *"It's great,"* he said, *"...but it's hearsay."*

Hearsay.

Bill's preface to the text-only *Ah Pook is Here* endorses the project, referring to the *"years of our collaboration"* and the *"more than a hundred of pages of artwork"* that were produced. Eleven pages of that artwork appeared in *Rush* magazine, confirming it as a published collaboration. Most of the other illustrations I'd produced for Bill had also been published and, together with those that hadn't, had all been initiated by him. It represented a volume of imagery that was *"unique"* as Bill put it, and he himself had referred to it in print on several occasions. In what sense was this hearsay?

Concurrent with Bill's exhibition at Track 16 in 1996, there had been what amounted to the definitive retrospective of illustrations *for*, and images created in collaboration *with*, William Burroughs at the Los Angeles County Museum of Art. Titled *William Burroughs: Ports of Entry*, it included more than 150 pieces of artwork. I'd gone there right after seeing Bill for the last time.

Despite the volume of imagery we'd produced together, none of it was represented. Neither was any of it referred to in the lavish 192-page catalogue for the show. My name wasn't even mentioned. Most incomprehensible of all, neither *Ah Pook is Here* as text or as collaboration were included in the extensive ten-page bibliography, filmography, and discography at the back.

In the acknowledgment pages of the catalogue for Bill's retrospective, curator Robert Sobieszek described the 'Burroughsian' themes that he felt defined the show. Included in his list were *"...apocalyptic visions, the abandonment of the distinctions among categories and genres, and the dematerializing of all concepts of reality."* From that perspective alone, *Ah Pook is Here's* prescience as an apocalyptic, prototypical graphic novel surely qualified it for inclusion.

Unaccountably, *Ah Pook* had disappeared. True to the life-imitating routine that had characterized it all along, it had itself become a lost book. It had simply gone down the memory hole.

If such a working relationship did exist, why wasn't it *here* as a matter of record? For anyone visiting this show, it would indeed amount to hearsay.

A book under these conditions was a worse idea than a gallery show. *Ah Pook* had had an emotional conclusion. That was why I'd "buried" it. Digging up the body again and describing how it got that way would amount to an autopsy. A couple of laughs along the way maybe, but the thing would still end up dead. Now I had the added problem of proving it existed at all. I tried several different approaches but always came to the same conclusion: there was no way to turn a failed, lost book into an uplifting project to work on.

It would necessarily involve *all* the issues that had led up to and followed in the wake of *Ah Pook,* issues that had long since been put to rest. I would now have to confront them all again. I'd watched over the years as my friendship and creative interaction with Bill had slowly disappeared from the record but I had no interest in redressing the fact. It had been a unique collaboration, and it was depressing to see it go, but it was only one among many. It was water under the bridge. Now, however, I would be forced to draw attention to that omission.

I attempted various versions of the book, but after a few months I gave up. It required a quality of insight that was beyond me.

But the body had been dug up. It wouldn't be a simple matter of reburying it and forgetting it had ever happened. An unresolved image is an irritation; *a pile* of unresolved images is a *pile* of irritation. The idea of *Ah Pook* became an obsession all over again. I was back in the book.

When I was sorting through the material I was reminded of the many practical as well as intellectual bridges I'd had to cross. In particular, I remembered the enormous amount of reference material I'd had to find. Included in that pile was the work of the two artists whose imagery had been key to the project.

Hieronymus Bosch was a given since *Ah Pook is Here* ends up in a version of Hearst Castle in The Garden of Earthly Delights. The other was the illustrator who was credited with first rediscovering and recording the remains of the Mayan culture. The half-dozen images I'd found in the book had inspired my own, but there was no indication in the text of who he actually was. The pictures were credited simply to "Arch. F. Catherwood."

I'd gone back to working on other projects by this time that involved many trips to the L.A. Public Library. Even though I'd given up on the idea of *Ah Pook* as a show or a book, I decided one time — on the spur of the moment — to see if I could find out more about him.

In the Art section I found one book: *The Lost Cities of the Mayas — The life, art and discoveries of Frederick Catherwood,* a fully illustrated biography by Fabio Bourbon published in the year 2000. Bourbon had traced Catherwood's entire career with corresponding examples of his artwork. It was the first time I'd really seen all his illustrations and the first time I became aware of his oddly familiar life.

For the first time in a very long time things, began to blur.

Like me, Frederick Catherwood was an English illustrator, and also of Scottish descent. He also went to art school in London.

He also met an American writer who happened to be living in London at the time: John Lloyd Stephens.

Stephens had contacted Catherwood on the basis of *his* artwork and they *too* had agreed to collaborate on a book together...

...about the Maya.

Catherwood met Stephens in Leicester Square. A few hundred yards down the road from Piccadilly where I met Bill. One 'square' over, as it were...

It was an interesting discovery, but when it came down to it — so what? As I read on, however, the correspondences became so unlikely that they were hard to ignore.

Catherwood also moved to America to complete the work — and, just as I had — slightly ahead of his writer partner...

In Manhattan, his first home — like mine — was on Houston Street...

He *also* had a studio in Tribeca....

Like me, he moved from there to Prince Street...

We both had children born in New York, and both of us were separated from our wives there. His son, also born in December, was 6 years old at the time — as was mine...

We both quit illustration there...

He subsequently moved to California, where he *too* became an American citizen. He while living in Solano County, me while living in Solano Canyon...

As artists we shared a particular image style: *panoramas.* In New York we'd both become known for it. Catherwood through his panoramic murals which he exhibited in his rotunda on Prince Street, myself through the panoramic images I created for television — while *also* living on Prince Street. Images that had led to a career as director and which were the reason I was now *in* Los Angeles.

It was all so unlikely, it seemed like a joke. There was even a punch line.

Ultimately, Catherwood produced a folio edition of their collaboration and wrote an account of their history and friendship together...

... an account that had been published *more than a century-and-a-half ago*.[48]

That I would somehow be duplicating aspects of a dead man's life was odd enough, but the nature of the coincidences and the manner in which they had been revealed evoked an even greater one.

In the first two sentences of *Ah Pook is Here*, Bill wrote:

" *The Mayan codices are undoubtedly books of the dead; that is to say, instructions for time travel. If you see reincarnation as a fact then the question arises: how does one orient oneself with regard to future lives?"*

There's no such thing as a chance remark.

The number of life-imitating-art/art-imitating-life crossovers this implied were almost impossible to disentangle. Once the picture had been drawn out, all kinds of quirky connections started to appear. The 'clincher' turned out to be right where Bill had put it more than 30 years before...

"...Hart and Clinch Smith have lifted a stone and found the books with a skeleton curled around them in fetal position..."

At the very start of *Ah Pook is Here*, when I was trying to figure out a color technique, I chose this sequence where Hart and Smith discovered the lost Mayan books. It ended up looking too much like comic book so I'd abandoned it.

What struck me as odd, as I looked at it so many years later, was my choice for Clinch's wardrobe. I'd given him a *red* jacket. What would a guy be doing in a jungle in a red jacket? Gray pants, white shirt, tan fedora with a dark band, a dark neckerchief and a *red* jacket — in a jungle.

On the contents page of Bourbon's biography, was an illustration by Catherwood of a European man, presumably Stephens, supervising a Mayan excavation. He was wearing gray pants, white shirt, tan fedora with a dark band, a dark neckerchief and a *red* jacket — in a jungle...

What's in a word?

What's in an image?

In the book or out of the book here, Bill?

And *which* book exactly...?

"The purpose of information is not to create order but to maintain chaos"

HERE

Dead Fingers Talk was the first thing that came to mind.

Through the medium of images I'd established a *correspondence* with a dead man. An artist long gone whose images had inspired my own and whose life trajectory was remarkably similar to mine. The implications were yet to be determined but the manner in which the idea had revealed itself seemed indisputable. It had been communicated through words and images. These *were* dead fingers talking.

Bill?

> *"Dead postcard you got it? — Take it from noon refuse like ash — Hurry up see? — Those pictures are yourself — Is backward sound track — That's what walks beside you..."*
>
> — *Dead Fingers Talk*, WSB

... and?

> *"Your death is an organism which you yourself create... Death is also a protean organism that never repeats itself word for word. It must always present the face of surprised recognition"*
>
> — *Ah Pook is Here*

...the face of surprised recognition.

"I want to meet the guy who knows how to draw me."
We were back where we started. The circle was complete.
"The purpose of writing is to make it happen."

Ah Pook is Here had realized its own premise. It had died and come back to life. It had confirmed the circularity implicit within its underlying idea and manifested evidence of the possibilities it had set out to explore. *It had invoked a dead man.* Its principal character had crossed the line from fiction into fact.

Ah Pook was actually Here.

As with any correspondence, a response was required. Under the circumstances there was only one answer that seemed appropriate or even possible: the simple confirmation that it had been received. An acknowledgement.

Like a reflection *in time,* there was this book.

The question was how to proceed? How to *address* such a response?

"...if you are not orienting yourself on sound factual data you will not arrive at your destination, or you may arrive in fragments..."
— Ah Pook is Here

But what now constituted fact? The information confirmed many aspects of *Ah Pook is Here* and clearly indicated a continuation of some kind, but the elements that comprised it were incomprehensible. The concepts of fact and fiction, past and future, were so convoluted and intertwined they permitted no tangible frame of reference. No sense of place. No means for orienting oneself.

Ah Pook might well be Here, but where now was Here? More significantly: who or what now was I?

Not only the narrative premise but also the *form* of the book had been realized. The view that had presented itself was tantamount to an unfolded codex, a panorama. A record of time progressing 'page by page' had suddenly opened to reveal a bigger picture — one that placed *Ah Pook is Here* and my own sense of self within a wider temporal context.

A codex, like any book, is a perfect representation of linear time. When it's unfolded, however, it becomes an *overall* image of time and, like any image, *order* of viewing becomes subjective based on the disposition of the individual viewer. There is no indication for direction whatsoever. Where to begin and where to go are entirely arbitrary.

But there does have to be a *first* step and the first step determines the direction. In this case, the *tone* of the response. The correspondence evoked an image of death, but it wasn't some goofy event in the Twilight Zone, neither was it morbid. My first reaction had been to laugh, but the gravity of the information didn't really allow for comedy. It was a dilemma; a confusion *between* two very different kinds of feeling.

Anxiety is the feature of all thresholds — the fear of making the wrong move, saying the wrong thing, taking an irrevocable first step. Invariably the decision is based on precedent but for a situation like this I could find no precedent. This was a threshold of a very unusual kind. I didn't know *how* to move. I couldn't *not* move. And I couldn't walk away.

Bill?

"...there are no right words. Death is a forced landing, in many cases a parachute jump... Focus attention. Look with your whole body. Pick your spot and land in the dark..."

— *Ah Pook is Here*

Not step then but *fall*. *Fall* into the threshold itself and *Observe* the *effect*. Let *go*. Give *way*. Allow the first thing that comes to mind determine direction.

Jungle.

"A confused or chaotic mass or assemblage... something that baffles, perplexes, or frustrates by its tangled, complex, or deviously intricate character."

The fictional Hart and his friend Clinch Smith searched for the lost Mayan books in a jungle. In real life, on the other side of the so-called line, Catherwood and Stephens had 'searched' for their Mayan books in the very *same* jungle... in *fact*.

Both of these expeditions had resulted in books being found, one fictionally and literally, the other factually and figuratively. Both were motivated by a conviction that these books existed and that within them lay the secrets of a civilization long since lost to the record. By rediscovering this culture they would essentially unlock the past in a way that would influence the future. Knowingly or unknowingly they would change the *perception of time*.

The ideas that initiated both these endeavors were the long dormant sensibilities of the Maya. Ideas that had inspired, prompted, compelled even, the process of their own rediscovery. The monuments, artifacts, and books that embodied these ideas were the means by which the Maya had attempted to reconcile the same sense of all-encompassing entanglement that defined their world. Through them, they had tried to come to terms with the chaos that surrounded them. A chaos both literal and figurative. A jungle without and within.

It was in that sense of Here that *this* book might be found.

If the Maya did indeed exist within a circular temporal worldview, their future would not exist *beyond* the present. Unlike the individuals in search of these ideas, neither would they have defined their world in terms of *finding a way out*. It was a self-contained, mutually reinforcing world in which time expressed itself as an ongoing system of repetition. It did not *unfold*. It did not move at all. It existed *entirely*, as a reservoir of confirmation.

The Maya were preoccupied with time. They studied and recorded it with a dedication and mathematical precision that was unique to the Americas. If they did not perceive of time as moving, they nevertheless moved within it. Traveling 'back and forth' between the remote past and future in a way that enabled them not to predict events but to confirm them.

This perception was not unique to the Maya. Many cultures — and individuals within cultures — have viewed time in this manner. Given the fundamental uncertainty that defines the human condition this is only to be expected. The ability to access *future* time, above all, is at a premium. The long record of shamans, mystics, seers, prophets, psychics, and clairvoyants reveals a propensity that has conceivably existed since humans became conscious of time.

It's a phenomenon we call prescience; the knack of knowing ahead. Writers and artists have also been known to access such information from time to time and Bill Burroughs was among them. He had the ability to '*write* ahead.'

The Mayan view of time corresponded to his own sense of life as a pre-recorded script — the word/image track, as he called it. A perspective he appeared to validate many times through his writing. If everything was already in place, it was his contention that these moments of prescience could be forced to occur. With the right methods it should be possible to break *into* the track and confirm what was *about* to have already happened.

To that end he'd devised Cutups: the process of taking existing text, cutting it into sections, then rearranging it. From these new configurations, meanings not readily apparent sometimes reveal themselves. 'Coincidental' associations that suggest other levels of significance, some of which refer to events 'elsewhere' on the track. As he put it:

"Cut the word lines and the future leaks out"[49]

It's a form of augury that literally cuts to the chase. Random rear-rangements of cards, coins, dice, bones, animal guts, etc. require inter-pretation. With words, the meaning is direct. You have the answer in writing. Future events can be held accountable to their word. Given that such accountability does occur, the concept of life as pre-recorded script gains credence.

In terms of 'fiction' there have been many instances of life imitating art that can be described as the ability to access events 'yet to occur.' *Black Abductor* was one such book that overlapped with *Ah Pook is Here*. Other accounts of calamities-to-come are also well documented, many of which involve ships:

Edgar Allan Poe's 1838 novel about a shipwreck in which survivors eat the cabin boy named Richard Parker[50] plays out in real life 40 years later when survivors from a shipwreck also eat the cabin boy — also named Richard Parker.

In 1885 playwright Arthur Law's fictional ship Caroline sinks, leaving one fictional survivor: Robert Golding. Soon after the play's opening, a fac-tual Caroline sinks, also leaving one survivor — also named Robert Golding.

In 1898, author Morgan Robertson wrote of the maiden voyage of the *Titan*. A ship considered unsinkable.[51] In mid-Atlantic, it strikes an iceberg and sinks with much loss of life. Fourteen years later, the *Titanic* sets sail — also in April. There are 3,000 fictional victims — 2,207 in real life. Only 24 fictional lifeboats — 20 in real life.

More recently, there are planes:

A year-and-a-half before the destruction of the World Trade Center Towers, the pilot episode of Fox's *The Lone Gunmen* featured an attack on the buildings by a radio-controlled civilian airliner.[52] An attempt that was thwarted in the script but one that featured images consistent with the POV from the cockpit of the actual planes and which correctly named Boston and New York as the two airports involved.

In a universe of enormous numbers, it can be argued that fictional, factual overlaps like this must necessarily occur. It's inevitable that once in a while, life and art will coincide. But identical names associated with those events are difficult to ascribe to chance no matter what the odds. *Titan* author Robertson went on to write a story in which Japanese planes attack Hawaii — in early December — many years before Pearl Harbor occurred and before such planes were even feasible.

Odd, remarkable, noteworthy or not, insights like this are hardly comforting. If the correlations do in fact substantiate the possibility of a predetermined script they inspire a sense of futility if not outright terror when the events that manifest involve disaster and human suffering. More significantly it points up the fact that no matter how accurate the skills of precognition it still requires the living of the 'interim' in order to substantiate its claims. Life has to be *lived,* regardless. You have to *go* to the future in order to prove the match and you have to have the claim ticket with you. Bypassing that formality is not an option.

Even though overall time might exist as some form of accessible reservoir, in order to be differentiated, it has to be experienced as consecutive narrative.

Because *"Death needs time for what it kills to grow in for Ah Pook's sweet sake!"*

Any consideration of death is necessarily a consideration of time. In the scenario proposed in *Ah Pook is Here,* life is the process by which time is *made* by virtue of being experienced. Given the appalling nature of circumstance that human experience entails, it's an inevitable short step to postulating a less than benign intention to that process. An intention Bill Burroughs called "Control."

Based on the evidence, planet Earth is not being run for the benefit of the inhabitants. If an overarching organizational system can be postulated, it is clearly self-serving. (If the enterprise has a logo, in all likelihood it's a burning child.) As Bill would have it, an alien entity entirely indifferent to the concerns of the *"human dogs"* necessary to implement its designs. Life is exploited and sucked dry of all possible resource — including time — by this vampiric Controlling agency, which forces the unwitting participants to assist in affecting its purpose and, by extension, their own demise.

Mr. Hart is one such human instrument of Control. The *"Ugly American who would live forever."* His methods: the appropriation of technological innovation for his own purpose; the removal of political and ideological opposition through media-orchestrated censorship, smear campaign, and brute force; and the promotion of a one-God, either/or, good-versus-evil religious mindset to aggressively condone his intentions. All operating within a deliberately fabricated state of disequilibrium, requiring an increasingly stringent curtailment of individual rights to sustain. The fictional embodiment, in other words, of the controlling methods of Western Judeo/Christian political ideology.

According to Bill, like all mundane systems of control, it contains within its methods the seeds of its own destruction. To demonstrate this, he considered the inevitable collapse of the Western model with respect to that of the Maya.

In light of the current 'End of Days' religious hysteria pervading the Western political, cultural mindset and the "End of The Mayan Long Count" in 2012, this choice was in itself remarkably prescient. His run-down of the controlling methods leading up to the moment of intersection that much more so. Though it was conceived almost 40 years ago, Ah Pook is *undoubtedly* Here now.

The book traced the evolving process of social, political, and personal censorship and the increasingly blatant methods of enforcement necessary to sustain it. An ongoing, totalitarianist trend evidenced by recent events. Today's 'Homeland Security' and the 'War on Terror,' have ratcheted this controlling dynamic to unprecedented heights. The threat of 'terror' now justifies Orwellian methods of curtailment and infringement of individual rights with promises of more to come. Surveillance is almost total, yet it's still not enough. As Bill expressed it in *Ah Pook*, such a process cannot continue indefinitely.

GPS, CCTV surveillance 24 hours a day, more and more cops, more and more security,[53] relentless word/image 'programming' and 'monitoring' through the media, results in an increasing behavioral conformity, political correctness, and identical, cultural, religious mindset. *"A uniformity of environment that precludes evolutionary mutations."*[54] But such a level of control in the long run produces a dull, homogenous, *non-resistant* human product. 'Stepped on,' in drug parlance, to the degree that ultimately there is only the milk sugar left. With I.D. chips inserted at birth, the process is complete. There's nothing left *to* control.

Without Control there is no Time to be had.

> *"Mr. Hart has a burning down habit and he will burn down the planet. Because the more control you exercise the less time you have in which to exercise it... When all resistance is removed then what does control control? Control needs time. Time in which to exert control. Now Mr. Hart has the world all sewed up at birth... And where is his junk?..."*

He wants to scare someone just press a button. No trick to that. So where is your cool blue junk now?"

"When you carry control to its logical conclusion you eliminate suffering. You are no longer inspiring fear in others and breathing it back as junk. You can now start kicking your control habit because the walking dead are not going to give you any more charge than a tape recorder. Yes they ran it into the ground too but they didn't cut themselves off with a habit as hoggish as yours."

— Ah Pook is Here

"They" — the Maya — did, in fact, run it into the ground, but it took the Spanish to definitively tamp it down. As a result, the subtleties and complexities of the Maya worldview may be lost forever.

In *Ah Pook is Here*, Bill Burroughs extemporized on the possibilities suggested at the time of writing — ideas he further embellished to suit his own purpose. Historical accuracy wasn't a primary concern since it merely provided a backdrop for considering the larger concept of *time*. As it happened, the great breakthroughs in deciphering the Maya language occurred as *Ah Pook* was coming to life in the early 1970s. One of the benefits of that new understanding would be that scholars would have a clearer view of the Maya methods for *measuring* time. It was from that understanding that the implications of 2012 derive.

With its wheels-within-wheels configuration, theirs was a uniquely sophisticated and remarkably accurate system, one that perfectly demonstrated the concept of prescience — and, by extension, the idea of a pre-existing script. It 'traveled' back four million years into the past, and in the future, predicted the precise year when Hernán Cortés would arrive in the Americas. It also predicted, much further in the future, the moment of apparent consequence that has now become imminent.

Unlike our Western calendar with its three-part (year, month, day) demarcations, the Mayan calendar had five. It's referred to as the Long Count. First known use of this system occurs around the 8th Ka'tun or 7:00:00:00:01 — 8:00:00:00:00 which originates from a start date of all zeroes equivalent to 3114 BC. The first number in the series, representing a 400-year cycle, changes according to the interacting cycles of the other four. When all four zero out, the first number is raised one. If the system is continued to the present day, we arrive at 13:19:19:17:19 on December

20th 2012. The following day — the winter solstice of December 21st — the numbers will roll forward to the 14th Ka'tun: 14:00:00:00:00.

The concept of the zero was a latecomer to the Western mindset and many still have difficulty adjusting to it. When more than one of them shows up in the calendar, it invariably leads to panic. Zero is nothing. People are afraid of nothing. Nothing is the null point of transition. Ah Pook's time.

Bible advocates attempt to allay these fears. World events, particularly in the Middle East, are a clear indication, they say, that the fire-and-brimstone, Hell-on-Earth days of Revelation are finally upon us. Salvation is at hand. The added feature of an astronomical event coinciding with these dates confirms the fact:

Also on 21st of December 2012, the sun will supposedly intersect the 'vertical' Cygnus Rift of the Milky Way and the 'horizontal' band of the ecliptic — in the center of a *cross*, that is. A distinct sign from 'heaven' that the end is nigh. The time has come when it will be determined once and for all, in the bloodiest, most horrific of ways, which Bible group has the most important imaginary friend.

In keeping with the overall sense of context the Maya now bring to the proceedings, the religious Mexican standoff that has held the world in thrall for 1500 years will finally be resolved — forever.

Panic is contagious. Even non-believers are sucked into the fray. Politics, economics, and ecology are also now seen in terms of ultimate collapse. Suddenly, 2012 has come to represent the possible mother of all 'Nighs.'[55]

Websites, books, movies, and documentaries began cashing in early on what could conceivably be the *actual* end-of-the-world show. Each of them determined to produce yet more convincing evidence and go on record for having said, "I told you so."

Bill's alien expert pal, novelist Whitley Strieber, was right up front leading the charge. In the cover notes for his book, *2012:The War for Souls*, he summarizes the event: "Every 26,000 years, Earth aligns with the exact center of our galaxy. At 11:11 a.m. on December 21, 2012, this event happens again, and the ancient Maya calculated that it would mark the end, not only of this age, but of human consciousness as we know it."

A somewhat cavalier embellishment of the archaeological and astronomical facts which now introduces the further detail of the precise time of day. That would be American time, presumably, although which of the four zones it refers to is not specified. Appropriately, the overall impression is that of looking down a gunsight, but one wonders from what point of view he is able to arrive at the "exact" center of the galaxy.

In his typical messianic style, Strieber inserts himself into the plot as a writer who suffers the mortifications of the flesh in order to bring redemption to the world. Over the course of 300 pages he confirms that God-fearing Americans are the only viable culture on the planet, that they alone are capable of confronting life-threatening issues of this magnitude, and that they will do so the way they have always done: with brute force.

Aliens figure large in Strieber's repertoire and, true to form, he adds an 'extraterrestrial' element to the upcoming conflagration. Moving on from the commuter gnomes in cardboard suits in *Communion*, his 2012 iteration is reptilian — proving, according to Strieber, that the Biblical snakes, leviathans, and dragons were real, have always been at war with mankind, and finally, now, have a chance of winning. A good-versus-evil comic book, in other words, utilizing Bible text and spurious scientific data to provide a seductive but implausible pretext. The Mayan Long Count is simply more 'academic' baloney thrown in to provide 'historical' precedent.

The movie *2012* makes use of the same pretext, bolstering itself with additional scientific 'data' and the element of global warming to further its cause. The "hook," as the director described it, that finally allowed him to make a modern day Noah's Ark movie.[56] Biblical precedent is evoked to justify Americans once again taking charge and saving humanity from itself. Suffice to say, God, giraffes, and the Queen of England 'berth' safe and sound on the Cape of Good 'Hope' to start the same process all over again.

In comic book world, playing fast and loose with the facts is fine but when science, religion, and archaeology are thrown in to 'authenticate' nonsense for mass-market consumption, it suggests a more insidious process. One that perfectly encapsulates everything Mr. Hart stands for. Strieber's book and *2012* the movie capitalize on the underlying fears evoked by current political and economic conditions, reinforce the infallibility of the Bible, Western science, and Western military technology, and, above all, confirm the righteousness of the particular American worldview that considers physical confrontation to be the panacea of all ills. Their effect is to prolong the cultural dynamic. To bolster the process of Control in which the controlled get dumber and the controllers buy themselves more time.

The battle against 'evil' cannot be won, simply because the concept of *good* relies entirely on *bad* in order to exist. Everything is determined by that which it is not.[57] In order for bad to be banished from the world, good would have to go with it. The only way such an idea can be removed from human experience is by removing humans altogether. By *truly* "ending human consciousness as we know it." Given the mind-numbing insanity that prevails, this is not such a bad idea.

It was the conclusion of *Ah Pook is Here*.

Having human sensibility mutate into a novel form of parrot say, or an elegant flying squid, hardly seems like a vision of Hell. Certainly not punishment. It's only religious indoctrination that suggests that all other life on earth is somehow inferior. The human ideals of care, altruism, and sincerity are all clearly evidenced in the rest of nature. Boredom, duplicity, and the need to control, on the other hand, are not. The added disappointment of *Ah Pook's* conclusion to me was that Bill, in his text-only version, reneged on that idea. The parrot, it turned out, was a 'treehouse' parrot with a steering wheel up its ass.

Maya *scholars*[58] contend that there are no references to "changes in human consciousness" in the completion of the 13th Katun in any existing Maya texts, either on stelae, murals, or in codices. Neither is there anything to suggest that an out-of-the-ordinary astronomical event occurred at the beginning of the Long Count nor that one will occur in 2012.

Astronomy *scholars*[59] contend that the 'cosmic' alignment in question *already* occurred in its maximum configuration in *1997* and that the sun will continue to make the same transit for the following fifteen years. It will resume an even more ideal position in *2030*. The sun however can *never* align perfectly in this way, because its path through the heavens, as seen from the Earth, lies more than 5 degrees *above* the so called Galactic Center.

Whatever the outcome, the current interaction between the Maya and Western Judeo/Christian mindsets is a poignant re-enactment of the confrontation that occurred 500 years ago. At that time it was a confrontation between two living cultures reconciled by force. By greater *fire*power. As a result, the Maya were obliterated. They were certainly accustomed to warfare — they were simply no match for an alien, more efficient form of it. But it wasn't only a confrontation of arms. A fundamental sensibility separated the opposing forces in such a way that only one could possibly prevail. It was, in the end, a confrontation between two very different versions of Time.

The Maya view, predicated on natural phenomena such as agriculture, the seasons, and astronomical motion, was circular. Time was repetitive and, to a degree, predictable, involving only the slightest of variations. Its interlocking system of mutually sustaining gears above all acknowledged the *interdependency* of life. A totality of experience in which everything contributed equally. To which everything *belonged*.

The European view, on the other, hand was linear. Time was perceived as a line, marked in identical increments, stretching into the remote future and distant past. Repetition was contrary to such a view. Events 'progressed' forward toward an ideal: a belief in a future in which science and reason would ultimately prevail. A changing and more efficient technology confirmed this idea, indicating that such an outcome was not only possible but inevitable. It was a dynamic of optimism directed toward a specific intention. And it was aggressive. Progress *marched* — and it marched with conviction. One god alone supervised the endeavor since its singular purpose was either being achieved or it was not. A religious system defined by either/or, right-or-wrong, good-or-evil.

A dynamic of progress is by definition based on increase. In order to validate its methods, it must constantly produce *more* over time. It must run at a profit. Life, as a result, is perceived as a business, a sole proprietorship in this case, run with the same sense of urgency and competitiveness as any other. Everything within the scope of the endeavor — including nature and human beings themselves — is viewed in terms of its potential for forwarding the agenda and is assigned a value accordingly. A value that is distilled down to a form that can be clearly recognized and exchanged. In the end, Progress is defined by a single, tangible abstraction — money.

To the Europeans, *time* — and by extension, their god — was *money*.

To the Maya, this must have seemed incomprehensible. Like the Aztecs, they comprised an overwhelming numerically superior force and could conceivably have defeated their opponents with ease. But in the face of this worldview, their gods failed them. They were hamstrung by doubt.

In a circular system, *belief* in a changing future is an absurdity. The future is, in a sense, pre-determined, resulting in a kind of passiveness and deference that is absent from a system predicated on progression. Since there is no single, overriding aim to be achieved, it allows for a spectrum of gods to oversee its various aspects. Many gods bringing subtle shadings to a time without direction, beginning, or end. Linear, mechanical time permits no such quality. No tick is ever longer than the one that precedes it. Or bigger, or heavier, smoother ,or kinder.

The human heart perfectly demonstrates this distinction. It also marks time incrementally and is without doubt the measure of life. But the measure is qualitative in that each beat is a direct response to the context in which it occurs. The rhythm changes according to the way time is experienced. It's both a barometer of time *felt* and an odometer measuring time *spent*.[60] By implication, it's also an indicator of time yet remaining — and it was this feature that may have held significance for the Maya.

From the evidence, the Maya were a highly sophisticated culture adept in mathematics, astronomy, architecture, agriculture, literature, and the arts. In seeming contrast, they also had a predilection for ritualized violence. Human sacrifice featured prominently in their worldview, which from the modern Western perspective makes it difficult to reconcile. Their preoccupation with the heart makes these spectacles particularly gruesome, especially when the records suggest the very young were sometimes the victims. Horrifying as they were, however, these events appear to have been more than a simple demonstration of power.

The intellectual expertise of the Maya was applied noticeably to the study of time. They traveled back and forth computationally over millions of years. When the human heart in its capacity as *reservoir of potential time* is included in this endeavor, the ritual of sacrifice becomes more complex.

The offering up of the heart suggests a form of bartering in which time is exchanged for time. The highly potent time of the young is sacrificed in the interests of the larger time of the group. A form of appeal, in other words, in which the great repository of all time is asked to take back some of the concentrated material and redistribute it amongst the living. There's nothing novel in the idea. Sacrifice of "virgins" and the "unblemished" has been a feature of many cultures. Prescriptions for correct procedure are a staple of the Old Testament Bible. The 'purest,' most 'attractive' and most sexually viable of any life form naturally contain the greatest potential for qualitative life expression. As time currency, they command the highest possible rate of exchange.

It wasn't the violence of these rituals that disturbed the Europeans. As Don Frey Bartolomé de Las Casas and the good Bishop Landa himself pointed out,[61] they would introduce a level of carnage the likes of which the Maya had never imagined. Neither did they have a problem with murdering the innocent. Greed, righteousness, and boredom combined to create scenes of appalling horror and misery for young and old alike.[62]

Human sacrifice didn't seem to have warranted especial attention at all — it was simply one more feature of a cultural worldview that was systematically being pilfered and destroyed from every angle. The irony in that process, however, must have given the clergy pause for thought.

Human sacrifice was fundamental to their own religion — the sacrifice of a perfect human being had been perpetrated in the interest of validating and extending their own lives. "He died that we might live," etc. It was the act from which their entire progress-driven dynamic proceeded. But their ritual was exalted; the Maya's practice, worldly and profane. From a linear perspective, a *thing of the past*. It simply wasn't the way things were done anymore.

From our point of view, it all seems reprehensible. The superstitious insanities of a time gone by. Following hard on the heels of these events came the Renaissance and after that, the Enlightenment. Then the Industrial Revolution and all the benefits of the modern age — the 21st century, from which we look back on the horrors of the past with a more reasonable, more informed, more *progressive* sense of self.

In year one of that century, however — nine months in, appropriately — an event occurred that shook that conviction to its core.

An unparalleled spectacle of violence was staged in 2001 in which a few thousand innocent civilians were again clearly *sacrificed* for the purpose of prolonging time. A ritual that was no less primitive, no less gruesome, and no less beyond the control of the populace than the sacrificial rites of the Maya. In the interest of global economics and the furthering of its geo-political agenda, the system of barter practiced by a 'barbaric' culture centuries ago was revealed to be as current and efficacious as ever.

The dramatic scope of the spectacle was designed to resonate with a Hollywood-indoctrinated audience, but its purpose and method were no different than they'd ever been — symbolically placing 'innocent' human beings at the highest vantage point and destroying them for all to see, then orchestrating the reaction of the survivors to further the agenda of the status quo — to make more *time,* that is, for Control to control.

Everything about it was right on the *money.* Even the pyramid.[63]

The World Trade Center Towers were the only buildings on the planet — or in the history of the planet, for that matter — to have been designed and arranged in such a configuration: large, stark, identical blocks, 120 stories high, standing side-by-side. If a number could be assigned to them, it would be 11 — a number that obviously corresponded to the date of their destruction and one that had earlier been capitalized on by New York City television station Channel 11 for its logo.

11 has numerological significance as the symbol of balance.[64] It represents the two opposing elements of the cross in their harmonious aspect. It is noteworthy, therefore, that one of the most extraordinary demonstrations of the human sense of balance was enacted between them — in 1974, high wire artist Philippe Petit crossed seven times from one to the other. The destruction of the site of this remarkable event perfectly describes the existential sense of *loss* of balance that ensued.

Whether consciously realized or subconsciously acknowledged, a greater blow to the notion of progress could hardly be imagined. Far from being the panacea that the one god of reason had promised, technological advancement suddenly became starkly questionable. Despite all the *going,* we apparently weren't *getting* anywhere at all.

The suddenness and scale of the violence and the planning and resources necessary to implement it evoked a sense of overwhelming powerlessness that was instant and unique to this generation. It brought into sharp relief the ruthlessness and efficiency of those that Control — against which there appears to be no recourse.

Sacrifice, the idea that the 'survival of the fittest' is contingent on the suffering of those who do not survive, is fundamental to both the Mayan and Judeo/Christian temporal worldviews. It is promoted by the current Controlling ideology through its religion, politics, *and* science as an irreducible condition of progress, the benefits of which are shared by all. As a result, it is accepted by all but in the profoundest of ways, is acceptable to none.

9/11 evoked this dilemma which now contributes to the existential angst that characterizes 2012 — the questioning of time itself, the way it is defined, and our sense of helplessness within the system it imposes.

It happened to the Maya long ago and in that instance their many gods failed them. This time it is linear temporality and its one god of progress that is in doubt. Arguably, both are untenable. It is in this sense that the correspondence between the Maya and Judeo/Christian world-views is significant.

Such was the premise of *Ah Pook is Here* written in by Bill Burroughs almost 40 years ago. A prescient vision in which the distinction between fact and fiction, past and future, would ultimately blur. A time when the many gods of the Maya and the one God of the Bible, would once again meet in fateful conjunction. Just as he predicted, two inherently flawed systems of Control would intersect at a crossroads in time and this time around — inevitably — both would be in question.

At that moment Ah Pook would be Here.

It was a *quality* of consideration that Bill was somehow able to *draw out* through the medium of words. A meditation upon two models of time that resulted in a view seemingly existing outside of either. It required a further step however to bring that fact to light; another view also *drawn* from without.

As it happened, the same quality of consideration that inspired *Ah Pook* was embodied *literally* by one other individual like no one else before or since:

Frederick Catherwood.

The process of revealing the Maya culture came later in Catherwood's career. Less than ten years earlier, he'd produced plans, surveys, and countless drawings of another architectural wonder that had also never been recorded. On this occasion he'd also risked his life but apart from a half-dozen small reproductions in a couple of publications at the time, most of those images — in a manner also suggestive of one of the ideas in *Ah Pook is Here* — simply disappeared.

In 1833, after a year of studying and recording Egyptian antiquities with the Robert Hay expedition, he set out on a freelance project of his own: he decided, against the advice of his friends, to walk into the Dome of the Rock in Jerusalem and simply start drawing.

This building, also known as the Mosque of Omar was considered the most holy shrine in the entire Moslem world next to Mecca. For an infidel to even enter, much less appropriate images of its interior, was almost certain death. Despite this, wearing an Egyptian officer's uniform and with his feisty young Egyptian assistant alongside, Catherwood marched in, sat down and began to draw. Within no time, he was surrounded by almost 200 incensed Moslems preparing to kill him, yet miraculously he was able to face them down.[65] He then proceeded to record every detail of the interior, and produce the only accurate plans known to exist.

If anything could be said to embody the convictions and contradictions of the three Bible religions it's the Dome of the Rock. The three are so entwined and entangled within its walls as to represent the ultimate image of ideological stalemate and confusion.

It was here that Jacob spoke with his God, where Solomon and Herod built their temples and where the Israelites located their "Holiest of Holies." Where Constantine's mother Helena discovered Christ's tomb and the true cross and over which she built the church that would later become the Christian Church of Holy Wisdom. Here, too, supposedly, was the footprint of Jesus, left when he rose from the dead. When the Moslems took charge, the same footprint was then accredited to Mohammed as he ascended to heaven with the angel Gabriel. During the crusades, the Knights Templar moved in. Then in 1187, Saladin restored it to the tenure of the Moslems once more.[66]

For six weeks, Catherwood sat patiently absorbing and recording the silent but voluble testament to these comings and goings. The images he produced were photographically accurate drawings, unique in the history of architecture, which would be exhibited in salons and 'conversatziones' all over London. But no publisher would see fit to publish them. They would languish in obscurity for fourteen years until Professor James Fergusson included a few of them in his *Topography of Jerusalem*.

It was these images and the sensations they evoked that occupied Catherwood's mind as he confronted the Maya ruins ten years later. Singular visions that he alone embodied as he began the process of uncovering a worldview completely antithetical yet equally inextricably intertwined. It was here that the opposing ideologies had faced off 300 years before. Catherwood was about to bring the image compliment to that moment back to life. He would subsequently encapsulate the *entire* picture. The same picture Bill Burroughs resonated with when he first conceived of Mr. Hart, and the same picture I was able to draw out by making images to match.

This to me was the locus of the experience — its center of *gravity*.

Drawing, by definition, is a process of extraction. A means for eliciting the nature of a perceived event. Whether the event exists 'inside' or 'outside' of the mind, this process of drawing out, is a *feeling* process.

A drawing tool functions as an extension of the fingers. A tactile device tracing surface and contour at a distance, and recording the impressions in a tangible form. It's also an emotional sounding device, in that it acknowledges feelings about the perceived event. The artist is drawn *to* it in order to draw *from* it.[67]

The nature of that impulse can usually be accounted for. On rare occasions, it can't. Sometimes, neither the event nor the attraction to it can be readily identified. Nevertheless, the resulting image evokes a correspondence that is experienced as — or *felt* to be — right. It reveals a connection to things not visible in the moment.

Things that can be felt and recorded without being seen.

At our first meeting Bill had asked me if my ability to draw people without knowing them had ever happened before. I'd mentioned drawing a boy who sometimes appeared at the dinner table. He looked like me but he always seemed angry. I was the only one who saw him. I asked my mother if I'd had a brother who'd died but she assured me I hadn't. When Bill asked me if *he'd* ever called, of course I'd said no.

Eighteen years later he did — at least my mother called on his behalf. She revealed for the first time that my father had been married before he met her.

There was a shift. A moment of alignment.

"And I have an older brother..."

"Yes."

This was the kind of drawing Bill alluded to in the 11 pages he gave me in our second meeting. In six of those pages, he referred to forms of the word 'draw' 20 times:

"Draw out the feeling," Hart had told his artists.

"...draw out and accentuate the picture."

"...draw out this cold sore feeling."

"...draw in the dirty pictures."

"...draw the dirty pictures and words onto Mr. Jones."

"...draw an identikit picture of this virus."

"...that's the picture he wants, so draw it out."

"... draw [them] in and out until you get THAT picture."

Catherwood was *THAT* picture writ large.

"You only use a pencil gun once kid," said Bill in *Soft Machine*. *"We'll be wanting two pencils."*

If drawing is a process of extraction then the pencil is the digging tool. An abrasive device that agitates a surface to express an idea. Drawing is a form of emotional concentration that directs the mind in a particular way. A kind of archaeological digging that reveals 'new' configurations of thought. Like a dowser's rod, it seems to know *where* and *when* to dig in order to access 'currents' of idea relevant to the digger. Unlike conventional archaeology, however, it has access to all time. In *Soft Machine* Bill continues:

"I'll say it country simple from Pitman's Common Sense Arithmetic the lead in this pencil used to be radium a million radio active years here in this pencil draw it all the way back now push this pencil"[68]

And all the way *forward*. A pencil is subject to an internal gravity. It is *pulled*. The artist is *compelled* to dig.

The fact that Bill associated time and drawing in this way augured well for *Ah Pook is Here*. It clearly represented a process to him that was also more than mere decoration or superficial representation. In an interview with Jürgen Ploog in 1986, he added:

"When someone wants to explain something to me I say, well draw me a picture of it. If you can't do that, then where is it? It doesn't exist."[69]

Or conversely: if it *is* there, then it *can* be drawn out. It just requires the *need* to do so.

"Mr. C. and his pencils" as John Lloyd Stephens put it, perfectly personified this process of extraction. He literally drew the past into the present. Archaeological rediscovery, however, wasn't the only reason he and his partner had journeyed to the Americas. There was more to the picture, and it, too, seemed to resonate with *Ah Pook is Here*.

Stephens had been commissioned by President Van Buren to explore possible railroad and canal sites in Central America. A job that he fulfilled to the letter. He, too. was a visionary. He clearly saw that the United States would soon extend its borders from the Atlantic to the Pacific, and that steam power was about to change the face of the planet.

In 1839 he crossed Central America from ocean to ocean on mule-back, alone, to determine the feasibility of building a canal there. His findings, detailed survey data, and impassioned written convictions regarding, not so much the feasibility, but the *inevitability*, of such a project, generated the impetus for the first railroad to be built across the Isthmus of Panama. He would become president of The Panama Railroad Company, which would make that inevitability into reality — a feat of engineering and endurance that took eight grueling years to complete and one in which Catherwood himself, having exchanged his career of illustrator for railroad engineer (drawing *lines* through the jungle), also played a part.

The last time the two men saw each other was in 1851. Catherwood was returning from the San Francisco gold fields where he had been planning the Marysville & Benicia Railroad. He crossed the Isthmus and met with Stephens before traveling on to England. In all likelihood they met in "Stephens's Cottage" — a landmark alongside the tracks. Up river from Chagres, just beyond Ahorca Lagarto — 'Hang the lizard.'

The two men who had met as writer and artist so many years before, met briefly one more time, then went their separate ways. They wouldn't see each other again. Stephens died one year later.

The last time I met with Bill Burroughs was beside the tracks at Bergamot Station. I didn't see him again. He died one year later.

> "...And they keep switching identities. Who was I in the last century? The steep slope down to the tracks. Here and there are stone steps overgrown with weeds and vines..."
>
> — *The Place of Dead Roads* WSB

What's in an image?

What's in a word?

Art, art not. Drawing, pulling, gravity, grave. Now here, nowhere. Current, flow. Influence, confluence, coincidence. Correspondence. Circuit. Current, present. Pre-sent. Past *before* us. Future *before* us. Giving way. Tidings.

The circularity implicit in the history of *Ah Pook is Here* now revolved within a greater revolution spanning five times that duration. From that time until now, the *quality* of nigh seems to have remained constant. All that appears to have changed is the scenery. But it too suggests a *quality* of circularity.

Frederick Catherwood grew up at a time when the English once again lived in fear of 'the End of the World.' Napoleon's unstoppable military machine, which had rampaged across Europe, was now threatening to cross the mere 30 or so miles of water that separated them. England was an armed camp. Fear of spies, terrorists, and anti-monarchist agitators was rife. A new government department had been formed on that account.

The Homeland Security of its day.

Artists and writers were among those who fell under its purview. 'Surveillance' entered the vocabulary. Protest was inevitable. English men and boys, maimed and scarred from the war with France, were coming home to face unemployment and social upheaval. The Industrial Revolution was under way. Luddites and proto-labor unionist movements confronted it head on, predicting the depersonalizing, dehumanizing threat that it posed to society and the family.

The Angry Brigades of their day

They were hunted down and shot or hanged. The market-driven juggernaut was unstoppable. It would roll over the English, making them slaves in their own land. Workers now functioned as mere adjuncts to machines. A commodity based on the same parameters of cost and efficiency. Women worked cheaper than men, children worked cheaper than women. Men were too costly and made redundant.

The outsourcing of its day.

Crime was rampant. Along with capital punishment, deportation, and military conscription for even trivial offenses, a more efficient method of incarceration was devised: silent prisons. Solitary incarceration for years — or life — without sound.

The Guantanamo of its day.

When Catherwood arrived in America, the Alamo had just fallen. Sam Colt had just patented the revolver, Louis Daguerre had invented the camera, and an obscure young man named Charles Darwin was on his way home from the Galapagos.

The end was indeed nigh.

In time with the times, Methodist founder John Wesley figured out that the *"the time, times and half a time"* of Revelation added up to 1836 and the Second Coming was also scheduled for that year. Others hauled out the number 666 yet again, to add, multiply, and subtract it in even more startling and arbitrary ways to corroborate the idea.

"Time, times and half a time" were, in fact, materializing in a far more direct way. Sam Colt's revolver didn't just reduce 'everyone to the same size.' It did so with the pull of a lever. In an instant. The camera captured a perfect image facsimile with the same kind of immediacy. Steam trains were reducing distance in a way that also *redefined* time. At 30 miles an hour, passengers were initially so unaccustomed to the speed that they were unable to focus on the passing landscape. Then came the telegraph. Instant communication over vast distances with just a series of taps.

Words in space.

The internet of its day

(The first message sent by Henry Morse when his Baltimore line was officially opened was *"What hath God wrought?"* Numbers XXIII, 23.)

Spiritualism followed hard on its heels, establishing communication over even vaster distances — often also with mere taps. Young women across America had suddenly, unaccountably, breached the barrier between the living and the dead. The deceased now revealed themselves in material form and communicated in a manner suggesting not only continuation but continuation in conventional terms.

Prior to leaving England, Catherwood had also witnessed a new exchange with death.

The rise of anatomical study and surgical procedure necessitated more and more cadavers. But an intact corpse was a prerequisite to resurrection. Having it dissected or dismantled was tantamount to an eternity of having missed the boat. The powers that be, anxious to encourage the means for alleviating their ills, but reluctant to allow their own corpses for dissection, passed the Anatomy Act and the Poor Act to move things along — essentially making poverty a crime and the bodies of the poor forfeit in the interests of science. Bodysnatching from graves became a new occupation as a result, with burking following inevitably in its wake. Certain enterprising individuals circumvented the burying/digging up rigmarole altogether by simply murdering the poor and selling their corpses fresh.

The serial killers of their day.

Death became marketable. A corpse belonged legally to no one but it could now be sold at a profit. The dead became a commodity for prolonging the living — or, in the bigger picture — the dying. Mary Shelley brought Frankenstein to life right on schedule to express the ironies and moral implications of the idea.

English attitudes to death changed dramatically. A more elaborate kind of funeral appeared to ensure the safety of the deceased while the less literally inclined, who didn't consider an intact corpse a prerequisite to heaven, opted for cremation instead. Or voluntarily donated their earthly remains to science, a development that the *market* was quick to jump on.

In the past, corpses had to be wrangled through legal and moral constraints. Now they were handed over freely to be sold entirely for profit. A tradition that remains to this day, with the added feature — which also had its beginnings in Catherwood's day — of quarrying the bodies of the living poor for 'expendable parts.'

The fruits of this new foray into Ah Pook's world began to be gathered into collections for permanent reference. One of the earliest and most enduring of which began at that time as Guy's Medical School in London. When it opened in 1825, a young contemporary of Catherwood's named Joseph Towne, was hired to make wax sculptures of cadavers. It would later become known officially as The Gordon Museum, Guy's Hospital.

Images take you back, that's what they do.

And 'forward.'

"If you consider reincarnation to be a fact..." was how Bill put it, a statement posed more as a question. One revolving around the notion of fact.

Reincarnation, as it's commonly perceived, is an emotionally charged subject for which there can be no conclusive argument for or against. It's a spiritual palliative evoked by the same sense of apparent meaninglessness and inequality that prompts other compensatory visions of afterlife. In the case of reincarnation, an elaborate system of checks and balances in which each completed life is compensated or penalized according to the conditions experienced, then returned to suffer the consequences of earlier misdemeanors or enjoy the pleasures previously denied. It's a personal conviction that cannot be gainsaid or disproved, since it is predicated on faith.

The correspondence with Catherwood has nothing to do with faith. Neither is it an anomaly — there are no aberrations. The discovery was a fortuitous arrangement of circumstances that allowed me to see something for which there happened to be documented, *tangible* evidence. The chances are, such correspondences may be commonplace. It's just that we are rarely able to confirm them. With the associative power of computers however, that may change.

Identifying coincidence relies on the ability to correlate data. With computers, the amount of available data is now increasing exponentially and the ability to identify temporal correspondence makes such a mapping process more possible than it's ever been. Information about Catherwood and Stephens — and Bill himself — continues to manifest as a result of a few original coordinates. This book might not have happened if not for apparently coincidental connections in cyberspace.

Computers are finally providing the means for charting the limitless expanse of our mutual inner space the way wooden ships began defining the physical parameters of our exterior world. The inner planet, as it were, defined by subtler tides unconstrained by the dictates of linear time. That journey is only just beginning yet already the patterns and organizing principles of synchronous events are revealing themselves. If there is a reason above all for acknowledging the events that occurred in *Ah Pook is Here,* it is to contribute to that endeavor.

"I am a mapmaker," said Bill, *"charting unexplored areas of the psyche."*

Hopefully, this book establishes a few more *tangible* coordinates, a few more dots, for someone else to join.

To view reincarnation as a means for perpetuating *individual personality*, is to conform to the primary directive of the Reactive Mind, what Bill described as being compelled *"To be THE."*[70] To be one thing distinct from all else. Singular, isolated, and vulnerable. Something that can be *controlled.* It's a fear-driven, death-oriented consciousness encouraged by that which would Control the ideas of others in the interest of promoting their own.

Both reincarnation and heaven enforce a sense of individual *ownership* of life by promoting a potentially painful system of personal accountability when that life is complete. It's a process of continually obscuring the present with a fear for a hypothetical future. Given that there are no clear 'rules' for ownership, it creates a state of psychological imbalance from which Control can operate.

The craving for immortality is predicated on the same dynamic. To be THE forever. A longing that holds the possibility of becoming the ultimate THE — that which is promoted by religion and relentlessly reinforced in all forms of media: THE CHOSEN ONE.

Reward and punishment are fundamental to the Bible, based on the idea that human beings are free agents enjoying some kind of odd dispensation that allows them to do things wrong, and therefore need to atone for it. When Bill proposed that "women were a mistake," it wasn't women *per se* that caused the double take, but the fact that it seemed completely in keeping with this idea — the same sense of *wrongdoing* that characterized Hart's Bible mindset. More significantly, it seemed entirely contrary to his own theory of the word/image track.

By definition, there can *be* no mistakes in a pre-determined universe — nor in an *un*determined one, either. Nothing we do can be contrary to nature. All there is, is, is and we're as much a part of it as everything else. Nothing is extraneous. To think otherwise is to conform to the Controlling ethic of separateness. Hart doesn't consider himself a religious man yet he is driven by such a worldview. Many current environmentalist concerns also proceed from the same perspective. That the so-called 'mess' we're making of the world is an aberration of some kind.[71] A *mistake* on our part.

The idea that breaking into the word/image track is a process that somehow circumvents or tricks this system is also questionable. It also subscribes to the idea that human sensibility is somehow operating on the lam from the rest of reality. In an all-embracing, predetermined worldview, cutting the word lines is itself simply another aspect of inevitability.

If we don't survive disasters, ultimate or otherwise, it has nothing to do with rightness or wrongness on our part. We are subject to conditions that simply preclude instructions on *how* to behave. Whereas an argument cannot be made against the possibility of reincarnation to those who believe in it, this fact alone undermines its premise. The system of rewards and punishments it proposes must be predicated on an unequivocal definition of correct behavior. Since no such criterion is provided, on the basis of what can we be judged?

In a reality, where no rules are given, what determines fact? What constitutes fiction? Facts are inherently false simply because they are always incomplete. At any moment they can *become* fiction. Conversely, fiction can *become* fact. The two ideas are in constant exchange. They can switch in a heartbeat.[72]

When I started working with Bill, Carlos Castaneda's Don Juan had made his debut, Lobsang Rampa was high in a kite over Tibet, and the "gentle, stone age" Tasaday had just been discovered. Three events — particularly Castaneda — which greatly influenced my worldview. What gave them their power was that they were said to be *true*. They were presented as *fact*. Now, many years later, Castaneda stands accused of never having met Don Juan, Rampa has been exposed as a plumber from Devon, and the Tasaday are acknowledged as a hoax invented to boost tourism. Each of these outcomes, however, does not detract from the wealth of instruction that the original perception conveyed. The primary effect of this 'factional' method of presenting information was to seduce readers into a particular form of attentiveness.[73] A focusing of energy toward specific states of mind.

As it happens, Ah Pook himself may have performed in this way. Maya scholars now rarely mention him. In the context of death and regeneration, it's 'God L' not 'God A' who is considered the mover and shaker. Ah Puch/Pook is a lesser figure known to the living Maya and possibly to the Maya of history but he does not appear on any murals or stelae. He does appear in the Dresden Codex and it was from that that Bill took his cue. A moment of insight that may have been right for the wrong reasons.

To be aware of that only now, perfectly summarizes the book's basic concern: the nature of discrepancy. The interim between Is and Is Not. Between life and death.

What is Ah Pook?

What is *not* Ah Pook?

That was the question.

Is *this* the measure of time? The reconciling of disparity? The evoking of pattern from chaos — patterns that then dissolve into redundancy as more are discovered? Is the information by which pattern is formed and sustained fundamentally specious? Its purpose simply to maintain chaos in order to enlarge time? Is this the Controlling system to which we are subject? Fiction into fact, fact into fiction. A tyranny that keeps us on a treadmill forever. Is the only means for alleviating the suffering that results to destroy the system altogether? To break the wheel? To truly end the human condition? Is the greater image of that tyranny the impossibility of such an idea? That 'end' is the only option, yet vested interest, the belief in the possibility of better, the acceptance of sacrifice prevents it?

Does our only hope lie in the planet destroying that aspect of itself we call *us*? Tomorrow, the next day, soon? Is this the deep craving that haunts us? Is this *Here*?

For me, the question created a focus of energy that was always *current*. Despite its apparent demise, the emotional investment and unique formative instruction it embodied made it an ongoing frame of reference. Added to this was the *need* to express it. The internal gravity that had prompted the idea to begin with.

Prerecorded "script" implies another interpretation of the word: *Prescription*, as in the means for relieving tension. Whether on the physical level of pain or addiction or the subtler levels of intellectual 'longing' and 'obsession' it's a key factor in the algebra of need. When the right words are arranged on the R_x, the drug is available. When the right words and/or images are arranged, i.e., *coincided* in the mind, the *idea* is available. In this instance, Ah Pook was quite rightly the "Croaker"[74] and Catherwood was the result.

It was hard not to try and assign a provenance to the information that prompted this book. An agency of some sort. An intelligence, even. Unquestionably, there had been a relieving of tension — "hearsay" was an irritation that would have long persisted without it. But something appeared to have specifically scratched that itch. Events had occurred in a manner that seemed to deliberately affect a particular outcome — at precisely the right moment.

It was a timely business.

Every idea is evoked by necessity and within every idea there is a propensity toward a particular result. In the context of a pre-recorded script, a result that is a forgone conclusion. The expression of an idea is not prompted by the past any more than it is compelled by its inevitable outcome.

From that perspective, the intelligence that scratched the itch would be the idea confirming *itself* from the *future*.

The agency would be Me.

ME 3

"... the purpose of writing is to make it happen."

—WSB

BOX 23

"When you talk to yourself," Bill used to ask, *"who are you actually talking to?*

Who's actually listening? And who, for that matter, is the 'me' that speaks?

"I was 22 when I started working on Cyclops. A month ago I'd turned 23.[75] *He found this amusing. "It's an auspicious number," he said, but didn't explain why."*

Coincidence was a defining characteristic of *Ah Pook is Here* and it continues to be so even though that chapter of the process is over. I began writing this book, for instance, at exactly the same age Bill was when I first met him. My artist son Orien was 23.

Even though Bill didn't subscribe to the idea of coincidences in the typical sense, he nevertheless incorporated them prominently in his writing. The number 23 was one of them. He credited his fascination with it to an incident in Tangier — one that involved a shipwreck *and* a plane crash.

A certain Captain Clark had told him that he'd been sailing without mishap for 23 years. That same day his ship was wrecked, killing him and everyone on board. The same evening, Bill claimed he heard a radio report in which an airliner also piloted by a Captain Clark had crashed in Florida. It was Flight 23.

It's a number that appears throughout his writing: *Ah Pook* begins 23 seconds before the bomb drops on Hiroshima, the protagonist Audrey Carsons is 23 years old and B23 is the virus that brings down the show. By default it was also a number I became aware of. In keeping with the idea of coincidence as personal inner signpost, I always kept an eye out for it.

One of these occasions involved Bill's assistant, James, someone with a heavily vested interest in all things Burroughs — including the number 23.

There were many aspects of *Ah Pook* that 'came true,' some of them involving the unlikeliest of characters in the unlikeliest of ways. James was one of them.

This book is an account of the *entire* history of *Ah Pook is Here*. All the events and individuals who I consider contributed to that process are included. To leave them out would amount to gaps in the record — to situations without a pretext. As Bill's assistant, editor, archivist, and friend, James played a significant role in Bill's life and, on occasion, James's relationship to me resulted in courses of action that are integral to the story.

One of the more significant of these occurred after I'd already begun this book and it, too, is essential to understanding the events that followed.

The first draft of *Observed While Falling* arrived in his hands without my knowing about it. Editor friend Ann had passed it on to the Wylie Agency and, as Bill's publishing representative, the Agency had in turn passed it on to James.

James was now lecturing in American Studies at the University of Kansas. He'd finally put to rest any idea of sibling rivalry by becoming Bill's legally adopted only son and was sole heir to Bill's entire creative legacy. James's position regarding all things Burroughs was now fairly undisputed, and his opinion regarding my manuscript carried some weight in terms of approval.

The 'green light' to would-be publishers that the book was 'okay' with 'The Burroughs Estate' rested very much on James's say-so.

His response came in the form of an emotional and often historically inaccurate, six-page letter. He *"loved"* the artwork, *"enjoyed"* the writing, saw no factual errors in the text. But he had one pressing concern: he was *"not at all happy"* with the way he had been characterized. He *"urged"* me to *"revisit"* my memories. The approval of the 'Burroughs Estate' therefore, was clearly contingent upon his perception of the way he was portrayed.

Given the obvious dilemma this posed, I *did* at that point decide to revise the 'offending' material. I rewrote the manuscript, removing every reference that could even remotely be construed as negative and eventually James signed off on it. This was editorial strong arming of the worst kind, but in the interest of seeing the book published, I accepted the terms. Having made the changes, I spoke with Jeffrey Posternak at the Wylie Agency and emailed James about moving the project forward. Even though Jeffrey had offered to represent the book once James's concerns had been addressed, I received no further correspondence from either of them.

In terms of a green light to a would-be publisher, this presented a seemingly insurmountable problem. This was not a book specifically *about* William Burroughs, but it was predicated on a complete accounting of the interaction between us. It was an autobiography, but in order to convey the significance of the collaboration, I needed to incorporate *pieces* of the *Ah Pook* text.

I talked to lawyers to try to clarify my rights. They responded with similar scenarios: I could include the text under the doctrine of fair use but if the Estate was not conducive to the project, there was still a case for dispute. A publisher would be unlikely to touch it. I could make a case for collaboration and 'joint authorship' but that would cost me time and money — a lot of money. I *had* no money and I was worn out.

I decided the project was cursed. The best thing to do would be to get rid of it. I would burn all the artwork and be done with it.

I talked with director friend Eric and made plans to film the event. He talked to a pyrotechnic expert and between them they figured out the best chemicals for controlling the burn and the best way to record it. I designed an installation for a video exhibition of the finished product, and made plans to bring all the material to San Francisco. It was a rational, thoroughly-considered plan.

But then Izzy showed up. I went to Ohio instead.

I'd overlooked the most important part of James's letter:

In the event that I was unable to adjust my memory to coincide with his own, James had included a parenthetical caution:

"(Also bearing in mind that a great many letters between all of us are preserved in Ohio...letters written by our younger selves and often very revealing)"

It was right there. Not the idea that such letters existed, but the place in the Ohio State University Archives where he told me they were supposedly kept:

Box 23.

It occurred to me there might be other information in Ohio I was unaware of, so in July 2007, I flew to Columbus on flight 223, took route 23 North and spent two days examining everything related to *Ah Pook is Here* in the archive.

As expected, the embarrassing letters were nowhere to be found. I did, on the other hand, find two letters I'd written to Bill that reminded me of what a great time-game *Ah Pook* had been. They confirmed the process of using photo reference for the characters and moving them back and forth in time and talked about our research into Mayan and Egyptian hieroglyphs. I was pleased to inform him I'd discovered an identical glyph from both cultures and was using it as a detail in the imagery.

I also found a series of letters between James and the English art director of the text-only *Ah Pook is Here*. After 30 years, the reason my cover hadn't "worked" would become that much clearer.

James himself had instructed the art director on what image should be used.

"As to a suitable picture of Ah Pook for a cover illustration I am making copies of a few images to send to you this week... As you know, many of the Mayan god-images can be found in full-color in various books, and I believe such an image could be very powerful and effective in getting attention for the book."

It could indeed. My cover wasn't mentioned. Neither had I been privy to any of these conversations regarding a book I'd worked on for seven years.

Most of the other material in the box was familiar to me, but amongst the paperwork, I found one folder titled "WSB Desk Scraps" that turned out to be especially enlightening. It was described as a collection of "newspaper clippings and odds and ends" that Bill had brought over from London. Amongst his little hoard of photos, bon mots, and aphorisms were several catalogues, business cards, and flyers from theosophist, spiritualist, and occult societies. Otherworldly reference he'd considered important enough to bring with him across the Atlantic.

I was in the right place. It confirmed my other reason for traveling to Ohio.

I had a date with Frederick Catherwood.

Sculptor friend Rebecca had invited me to stay with her in Columbus. She happened to live a couple of miles from the OSU library. When she heard about Catherwood, she insisted we drive to Lily Dale, "the world's foremost spiritual community" in upstate New York. It was a couple of miles from where she grew up.

I'd never heard of the place, much less thought about going there. It was an intriguing idea, even so: a Harry-Potter type community of mediums and spiritualists that had been patronized by the likes of Mae West, Arthur Conan Doyle, and the Roosevelts. And it was only a four-hour drive from Columbus. Why not?

Rebecca was far less casual. *"Why do you suppose all these things are so convenient?"* she asked. *"It's a signpost. Are you paying attention?"*

Since I'd discovered Catherwood's life story, I'd searched for more information about him. I'd read the two bios by Victor von Hagen (who described Catherwood's writer partner, John Stephens, as a man whose career was determined by "accident."[76]), contacted Maya/Catherwood scholar Professor Angela Thompson at East Carolina University (who described Catherwood as a man dogged by a "poltergeist."[77]), and I'd checked all the publications I could find in libraries and online. I'd also uncovered many details that had not as yet been published.

The more I found, the more I became fascinated by the man himself. Naturally, I was curious to know what he looked like. As it happens, so were his various biographers.

Despite Catherwood's celebrity status on both sides of the Atlantic, and his friendship with some of the greatest painters, writers, and historians of his time, no portrait or even written description of him is known to exist.[78] At a time when just about anyone who was anyone was having their portrait sketched or exchanging copious letters and diaries with one another, nobody apparently had felt compelled to describe the enigmatic Mr. C. I found this not only incomprehensible but unacceptable. He'd inspired the imagery for one book and the words for a second. Not knowing what he looked like was out of the question. *THAT* picture must surely exist. It had to be drawn out.

I'd already started working on it by the time I got to Ohio. The usual method of researching someone by trying to get inside their head was a given under the circumstances, and so far it was uncovering all kinds of new data. Coincidence was key to this process and, as Rebecca pointed out, there were a lot of them around.

One of the more intriguing details of Catherwood's life was his death. After supervising the folio publication of his collaboration with Stephens, he set out from England across the Atlantic en route to California, where he intended to rejoin his son and continue work on the Marysville & Benicia Railroad. He would never arrive.

Throughout his life, Catherwood had the uncanny knack of being noticeably present during significant events, while being equally noticeably absent in the record of them. Appropriately, in the newspaper accounts that followed the shipwreck, his name alone was absent from both the survivors' and the victims' lists.[79]

The *Arctic* was one of the first trans-Atlantic steamers. It had collided with another ship in heavy fog off the coast of Newfoundland. The number of victims incurred made the tragedy the benchmark for loss of civilian lives at sea. Fifty years later, the *Titanic* would claim that title, a fact I was well aware of given my earlier fascination with the event. Unlike the *Titanic,* however, the *number* of lifeboats was not the issue.[80] The crew had simply commandeered them, leaving all of the women and children and most of the male passengers to drown. There were 282 passengers in total.

Only 23 survived.

My question when I arrived in Lily Dale was whether Catherwood had been one of them — an extremely obscure question that I did not hint at in any way, to anyone. I met with a medium, one-on-one, whose name I'd selected at random from the Lily Dale telephone directory.

Her response was simply a reaction to our sitting across from one another. It made the hairs on my arms stand on end.

"There's a man," she said. *" He's in a fog."*

She then flattened her hand as if to make a salute, but placed it under her nose and pushed her head up.

"Like this," she said. *"His body is below — underneath."*

She swept her hand toward the floor.

"You understand? He's trying to shut out those around him. He doesn't want to acknowledge them. He just wants it to end.[81] *That was his passing, you understand."*

"He's here with you."

Who was "he" and who was "you" here? And where, exactly, *was* "here"? From where was this information being retrieved? The medium had indicated the space to the left and behind me.

"Back," she said. *"Far back..."*

Back in time that is, not space. What kind of exchange was this that could raise the hairs on my arm?

Despite the obscurity of the undisclosed question, over the course of an hour it would be 'answered' in a manner that was as impossible to explain as it was to dispute. These were only the first of many seemingly relevant remarks. Remarks that would again create the stumbling block to the idea of 'mere' coincidence.

Prior to leaving for Ohio, I'd ordered a copy of *Women and Children Last,* an account of the wreck of the *Arctic* by a descendant of one of the survivors.[82]

It was in the mailbox when I got home.

As a result of my trip, reading the descriptions of families drowning in the icy darkness of the Atlantic was hard to deal with so I gave up. As I was closing the book, however, I noticed a timeline of the event in the back. It said that in November, two months after the shipwreck, a single empty lifeboat from the *Arctic* had been found floating off the coast of Newfoundland. The oars were still in the boat but there was no clue as to the fate of its occupants.

It was discovered by the schooner *Lily Dale*.

Once this reciprocating process is acknowledged, it's difficult to disavow it.[83] The nature of the informational exchange may be impossible to explain but its effects are impossible to ignore. My brief encounter with a stranger in Lily Dale questioned, above all, the *location* of such information. The vague literal idea that it was being accessed from 'beyond' hardly seemed adequate. It was right there *between* the two of us. "Between," however, was not confined to the space directly in front of us. It was all around us.

I'm familiar with cold reads and the ability to make quick assessments of character. I'd presented the medium with many clear signs of what kind of person I might be. The information she elicited on my behalf, however, was so 'outside' the likely parameters of such an assessment that it couldn't be dismissed that easily. The very obscure question, which I had not revealed, was not one that my appearance or demeanor could have suggested.

If it were possible that something so remote could be accessed by a kind of self-deluding mental sleight-of-hand then it was a trick I wanted to know about. If not — if this data existed in a location that confirmed that there was indeed more to "myself" than was readily apparent — then I wanted to know about that as well. Whatever the answer, I couldn't lose. I decided to try one more consultation, this time with someone closer to home.

My west coast medium was recommended through a series of random connections. She was described as a woman with a *"very high success rate"* and *"discreet beyond discreet."* I met with her in December 2007 in San Francisco.

She sat behind a small desk in a corner of a sparsely furnished room clearly dedicated to this kind of work. Once again I told her I had a question but that I preferred not to divulge it. It was a very different kind of question this time and not specific to an individual. I simply wanted to know how I could learn more about the process. How I could access the information myself.

She handed me a *pencil* and a small piece of paper and told me to write my name. She then took the piece of paper and, without looking at it, pressed it between her palms. A few moments later she reached for the tumbler of water on her desk, lifted it, then very carefully lowered it again, in a manner that was strangely evocative.

"This is familiar to you," she said, a question posed more as a statement.

I shrugged.

"It's not water, right? Well, he wants you to know he doesn't need it anymore."

"What does *he need?"* I asked.

No answer.

" Shooting guns. I see him shooting guns..." she said.

She made the standard pointing index finger image of a gun and 'fired' it back and forth across in front of me.

"...ONE OF HIS FINGERS IS MISSING."

"He's a sincere man. He has a unique sense of humor. Male humor. He's with you on what you're doing. He was a scrapper — he'd take on anyone. Not literally, of course. — You've traveled a long way for this project — I don't want to know what it is. I don't need to know what you do. — Obstacle — Deliberately obstructed. You've been suppressed. A brick wall. A couple of years ago. He uses an expletive. Buddy, he says. He'll help you. He'll do what he can."

"How can he do that?"

No answer.

Her demeanor then changed. *"You'd like to know more about this, I'm thinking — how it works, I mean."*

She gestured to several fold-up chairs at the back of the room.

" I do give seminars but that wouldn't work, would it? — with you being so far away. Maybe we could arrange something over the telephone."

I took her up on her offer and spent an hour a week for the next six months learning not about the 'tricks' of medium-ship, but the underlying philosophy of *attention* she applied to her life. In that time I came to know her as a friend. Her sincerity to me was beyond doubt.

As a result of an apparent obstruction and a diversion through a university archive, I'd been drawn to another point of view, another kind of attentiveness. The effect of those six months would be to *add* to the process, not detract from it. It wasn't *about* answers but further clarifying the question.

I'd established a *correspondence* with a dead man. How should I *address* the response?

The key was in simple acknowledgement, my west coast medium had informed me. To be in the *same place* at the *same time*. To focus on the question and allow its *whereabouts* to reveal itself. To not inhibit or qualify the response but to let it flow. Let the *first* thing that occurs to you have its say.

In that she gave me remarkable insight.

"And no matter where *you are,"* said Bill, *"write it down!"*

As a result of Box 23, I borrowed money and kept going. I followed Frederick Catherwood through the Bancroft Library, Los Angeles Library, UCLA Library, Cambridge University Library, The British Library, and the British Museum. I talked with Mayan experts, Burroughs experts, and experts on the paranormal. I traveled through 19th century London, Rome, Athens, Cairo, and Beirut. From there to old New York City, the jungles of Central America, and the gold fields of San Francisco. I came a lot closer to THAT picture.

I also came closer to Ah Pook.

The project had increased in scope, expanded in time. It had confirmed Bill's prescience as a writer and my own contribution to that process. It was to Me an interaction worthy of note.

But if *Ah Pook* had been ahead of its time when it started, the time it was ahead *of* was now approaching. In order for this book to be relevant it needed to be published in sync with the intersection it had anticipated — 2012.

I *had* written it down, but the *words* were getting me nowhere.

NEW YORK

The Salomon Arts Gallery, at 83 Leonard Street in Manhattan, is one block south of Franklin Street. Being on the fourth floor, the windows look directly into the back windows of 77 Franklin, ten feet away. I wasn't aware of the exact proximity until I arrived in New York to mount the show. (Choosing an art gallery in New York based on its precise location in time and space is hardly an option). Nevertheless, the revived artwork would be shown for the first time a few feet from where it had come to an end, 30 years before. The following year, 2009, it was shown at Track 16 in Los Angeles, the last place I'd seen Bill.

When it became clear that the Burroughs Estate would not promote the collaboration of *Ah Pook* nor encourage this book, I decided to let the images speak for themselves. By making them public I could at least remove the notion of hearsay and conceivably interest a publisher.

Gary Groth contacted me as a result of the L.A. show. Even though he'd been publishing graphic novels, comic compendiums, and illustrated books for nearly 30 years — *and* was a Burroughs fan — he was *"...ashamed to admit [he'd] never heard of the project."* It was a reaction I was more than familiar with. Having read the then-current version of *Observed While Falling*, he agreed to publish it.

In his opinion however, anyone reading about the long history of a word/image collaboration would want to see the collaboration itself. He suggested printing *Ah Pook is Here* as it had originally been conceived. In its incomplete form, it would be a work-in-progress frozen in time. Rough drawings, finished paintings, and notes, etc., together with images of Bill's annotated manuscript would show what the collaboration had tried to achieve. The Calder text would be included as a standalone piece in the form in which it had been published in 1979. The two books would then be produced together in a box set.

It was a nice idea but inevitably it revived the issues that had confronted it six years before. Despite the sincerest of intention and reasoned argument, Gary would not prevail. In the course of the discussions he unwittingly uncovered even more reasons for discouragement.

When I first received a copy of the Calder *Ah Pook,* I'd only briefly skimmed through it. I knew the text by heart — why would I actually read it? In the course of clarifying it for this new iteration, however, I had to read it word for word. It was only then that I would discover the oddest of details in the mystery of my disappearing cover.

Not only had my image been replaced, but the section of text it referred to had been *removed.* As it happened, the *only* section to be edited from Bill's working script.

I'd chosen that section for the cover because it perfectly encapsulated the progress of the "Ugly American," from Mexico to Los Alamos and the colonization of space. It was a wonderful panoramic sequence that essentially summarized the premise of the book. It also introduced and explained the title character.

The editor was James.

No one would ever see this discrepancy. After 11 months of negotiation, the Burroughs Estate would not agree to the project. James would not allow *any* of Bill's text to be published in the form for which it had been intended. He gave no reason.

The alternative was to produce a book of the artwork without Bill's text. Thirty some years ago, the words had been published without the images, now it would be the reverse.

"Between" had characterized the process all along: an interaction between writer and artist, fact and fiction, past and future; a book that was "neither one thing nor the other." Now circumstance had again come *between* the words and images.

This could be perceived as unfortunate. To consider it in those terms, however, would be contrary to the idea. In a pre-recorded script there can be no *un*-fortune. Separation had merely sustained the possibility for further dialogue. It had allowed the space for interaction to continue.

In this, its current iteration, *Ah Pook is Here* has achieved its essential purpose. It has realized its own idea.

Like the fragment of the Mayan codex that inspired it, the images have been separated from their textual narrative by the instrument of Control. In effect, the line between fact and fiction, past and future, has been incontrovertibly blurred.

The book has *"happened."*

QED.

The words and images of *Ah Pook is Here* will now be separated indefinitely. Writing is a timely business.

Time is up.

As I was taking down the New York gallery show to drive it out to L.A., friend Max gave me a copy of Bill's *Last Words*. Holed up during a blizzard in Oklahoma, I read it from cover to cover for the first time. It's hard to imagine how many books Bill Burroughs read in his lifetime, but his final journal entry on July 30th 1997 — three days before he died — recorded the last. It began:

"Reading Titanic by Charles Pellegrino. Page18..."

When I got back to L.A., naturally I went to the library and found the book. The full title was, *Her Name, Titanic*. On page 18 the author wrote —

> *"Telepresence is the ability to share. What is an experience if it's not shared? You know, it's one thing to be wowed and zapped, but it's another to turn to a person and say "Wasn't that great?"*
>
> *"Sharing. That's the concept of an epic journey. I think the epic journey is part of our lives. It's part of human development in literature and exploration and everyday life. The journey's goal is to attain truth, a new knowledge. But unless it's brought back and shared, the journey isn't complete."*

In his second book on *Titanic*,[84] Pellegrino's first lines read:

> *"AND YOU ASK ME,* (author's caps) *why do I not believe in psychic events?*
>
> *How can I not believe? you may ask given what I have seen, what I have learned.*
>
> *And it occurs to me that I cannot provide for an adequate answer, because I do not believe the proper words exist for me to explain my agnosticism. You cannot know, therefore, and neither it seems can I."*

Just pay attention and follow the signs. Right, Bill?

Among those traveling aboard the Titanic were: a Mr. Burroughs, a Mr. John Hart, and yes — a Mr. Pook. All three of them drowned.

"Who is someone you have known?'
"Who is someone you have not known?"

There *are* no answers.

There *is* no way out of the jungle. The end is also the beginning. The center — which is not a center — is where we always return, our four faces peering out into the incomprehensible tangle that surrounds us — one that sees it as it is, with eyes open; the second as it dreams it, with eyes closed; the third as it rearranges it in the mind of the imagination; and the fourth as it sees it in time.

A pyramid.

We are the tenuous sum of its parts. There is a moment of sunlight and shadows, then we are absorbed back into the question.

It is an image of correspondence.

A pattern.

A map.

An emotional glyph.

A chord that resonates.

I've been granted a wide tour of my confinement, Mr. Pook, now I'm back. It was a distraction of sorts, I admit, less a feeling of inertia, but what did I gain? More time? I think not. Better time? Maybe.

Was it worth it?

The Mayan codices *are "books of the dead."* They're the battered legacy of millions of human souls long gone. Consideration of the *"directions"* implicit within them *did* result in *"time travel."* Ah Pook is Here spanned decades and culminated in an event that sent me 'back' 150 years to another version of 'myself' confronting the Mayan god of death. Another artist face-to-face with mortality.

In that encounter lay the ultimate realization of the book's intention. The most compelling, incontrovertible instance of reciprocating fact and fiction. In *Ah Pook is Here,* the protagonist Audrey Carson interacted with a version of himself in past time to affect events in the present. In real life the *correspondence* with Frederick Catherwood functioned in precisely the same way. On both occasions, books were the currency of exchange, the means for travel. Through the medium of words and images, Catherwood came "forward in time" to set in motion the events that would lead to this book and the revitalization of the process of collaboration.

The evidence of that encounter and its resonance with the other insights that occurred reordered my sense of time and the nature of creative impulse. It gave credence to the notion of the word/image track and the inevitability of the events that led to such a conclusion.

From that perspective, my working with Bill Burroughs had also been inevitable. It was the luck of the draw but the drawing had long since been made. I'd merely been in the appropriate place at the appropriate time. *Fallen* into place, that is,[85] as every moment in such a scenario must necessarily do. An idea that by no means diminishes the experience, since the *Observations* remain the same.

In the case of Bill Burroughs, I was afforded insights that are unique to my experience. They revealed the possibilities of collaboration and the potential of word and image working together. Possibilities that are that much greater when the Word comes from Bill. *Inevitably*, I acknowledge the effect of that interaction.

One of his many words of advice through the years was that, "*No organism in the history of the planet ever did anything unless it absolutely fucking had to.*" In that remark, he characterized my debt to him: his authenticity compelled me to look. Sometimes I agreed with him, sometimes I didn't, but in the process of looking, I became aware.

Testament to that idea is the fact that years after he'd gone, I was afforded the greatest insight of all: I actually got to see the Martian's arm. How long it is, I've no idea. Very long, obviously. Hundreds of years at least. But then I only got a glimpse of it.

For that privileged moment, Bill, I thank you.

Mr. Hart original drawing

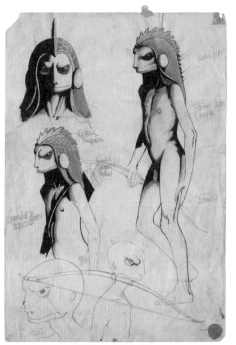

Cumhu the Lizard Boy

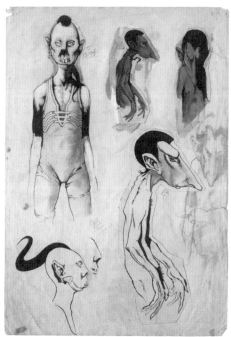

The Dib and Jimmy the Shrew

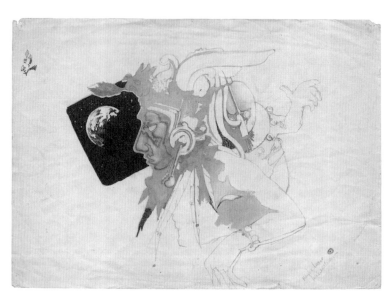

The Corn God

Virus concept sketches

Mayan God specs

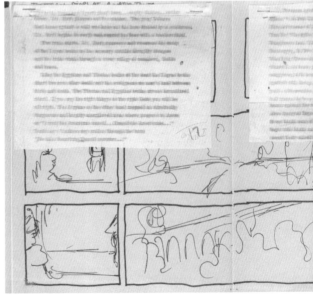

Book mock up

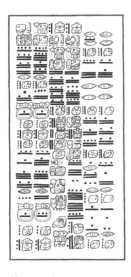
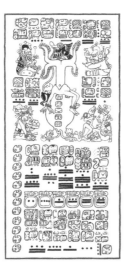

Mayan codex copy

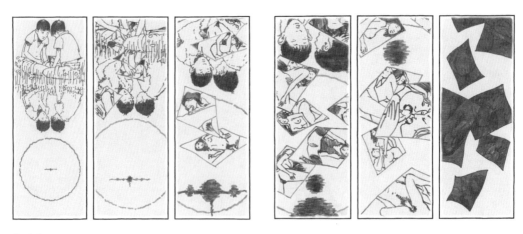

Control...

The Books are found...

The Gods escape...

Mayan city...

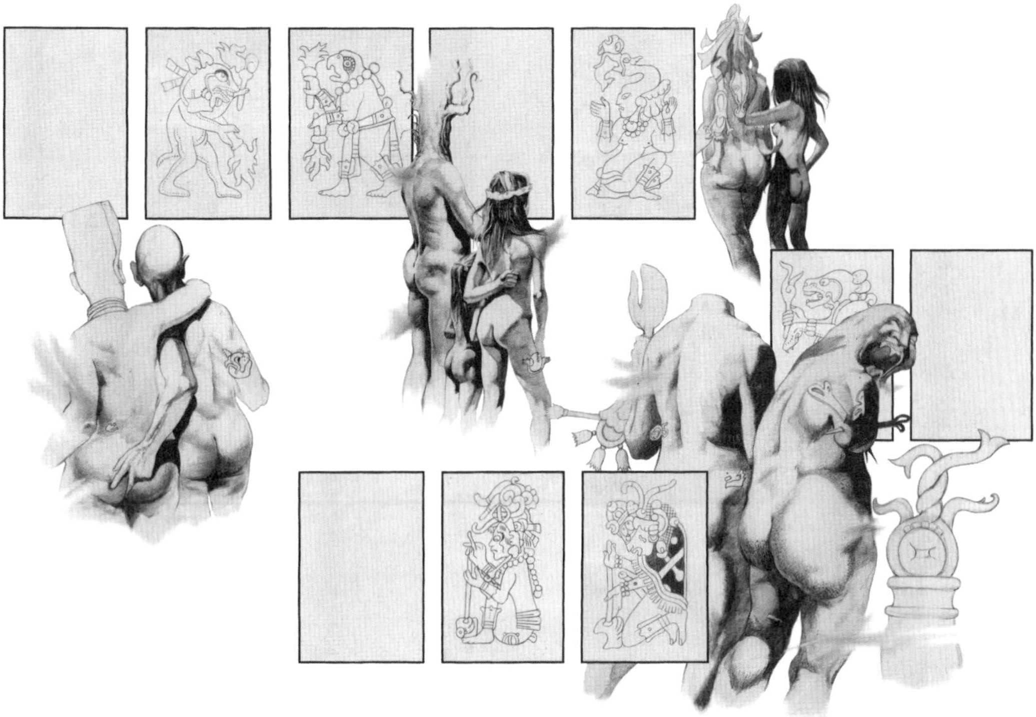

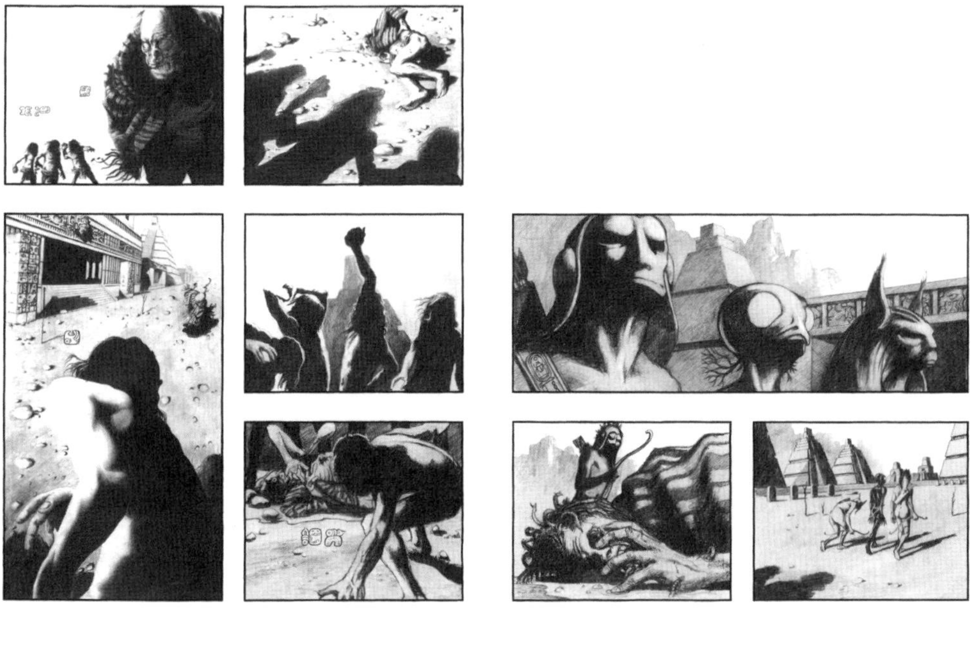

Mayan city...

Future trip...

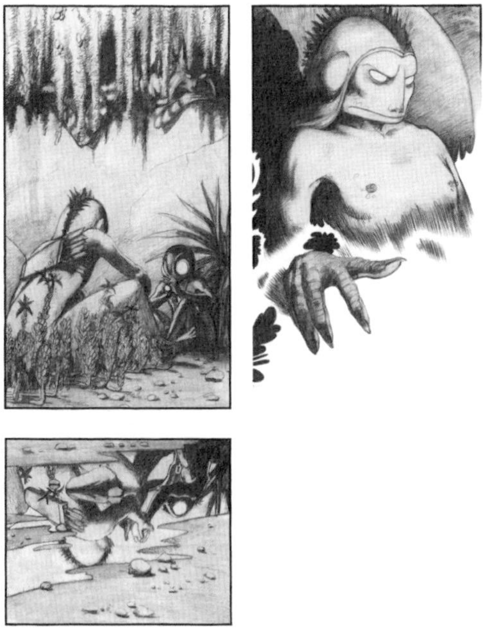

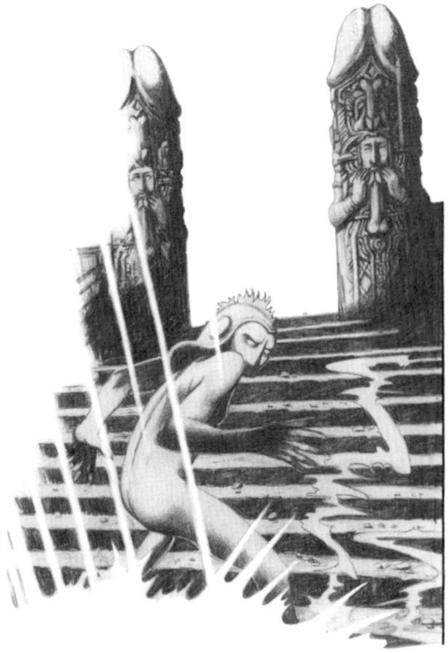

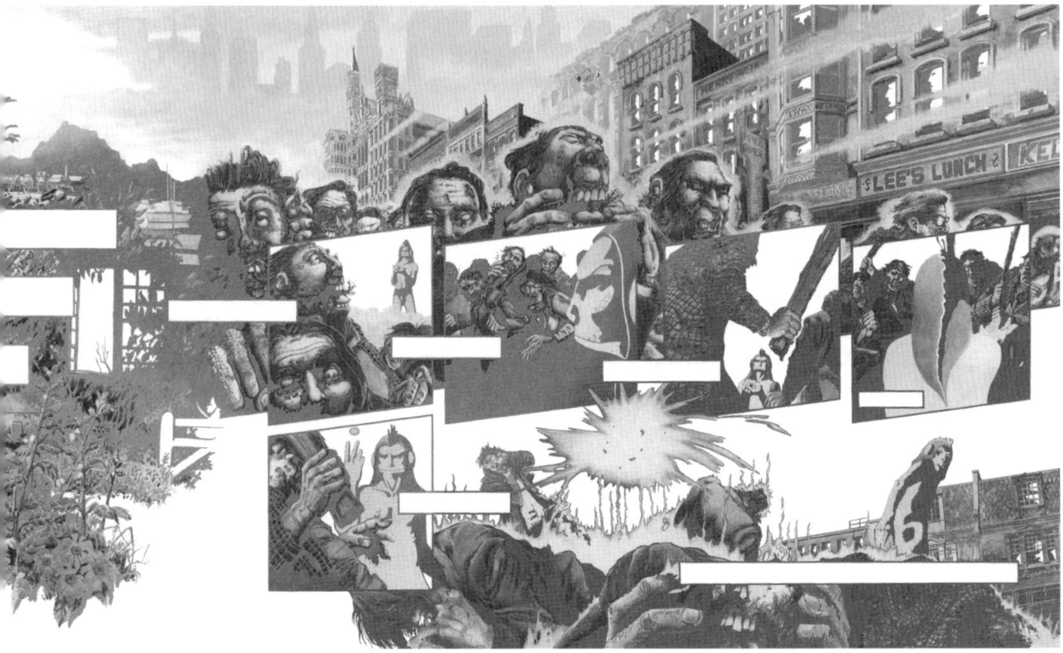
LEE'S LUNCH

Future trip... Eros...

Garden of Delights sketches...

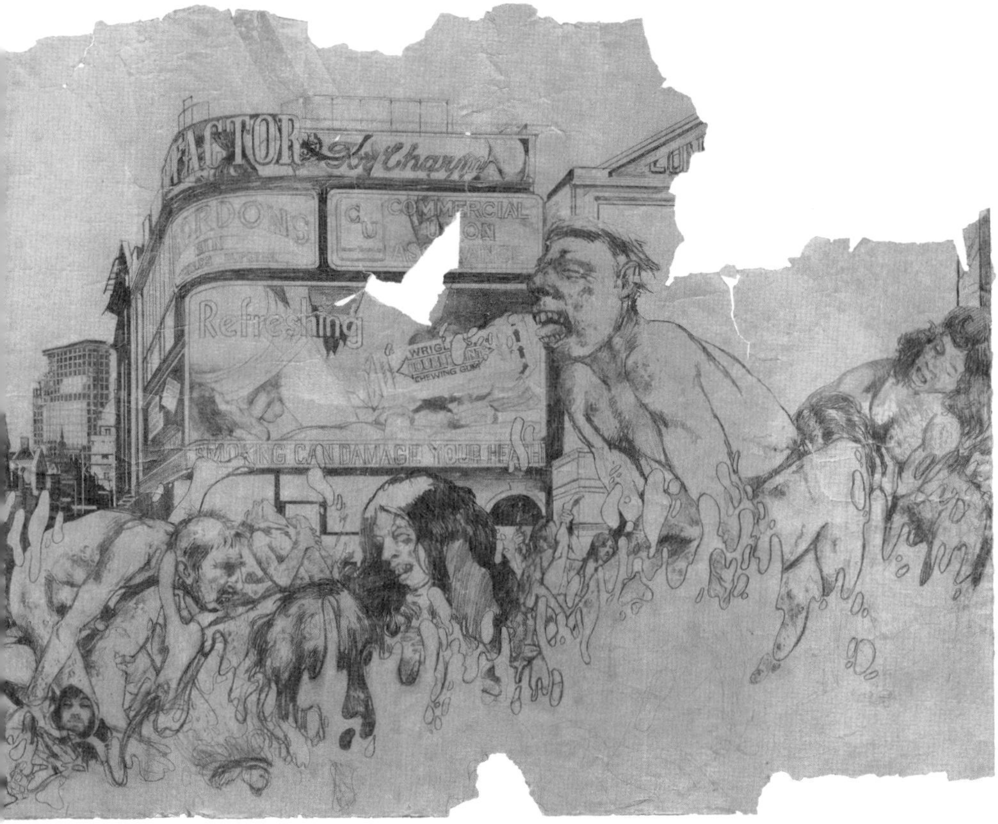
COMMERCIAL
Refreshing
CHEWING GUM

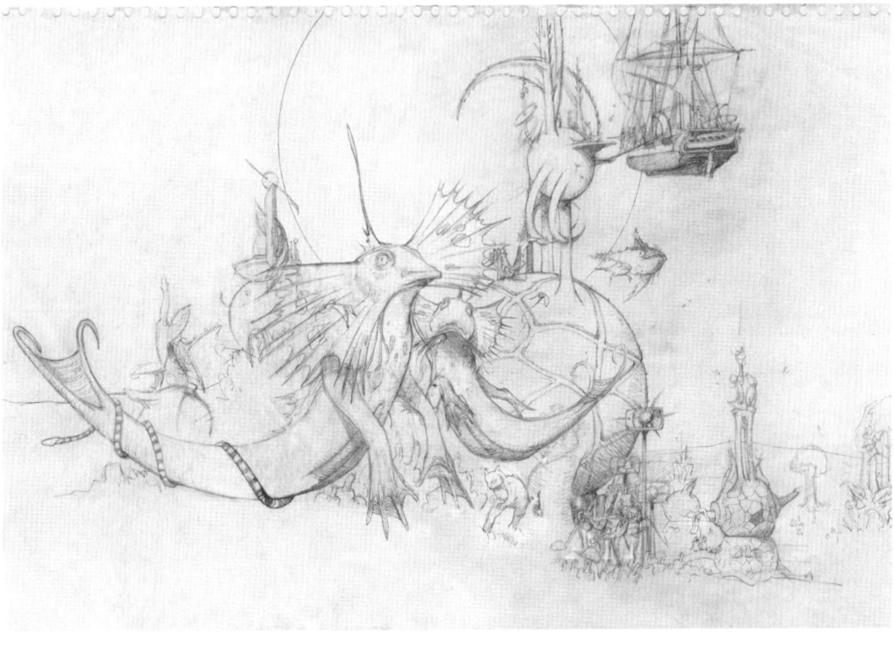

Percy Jones

The biologic store is now open...

Audrey and The Dib in the city

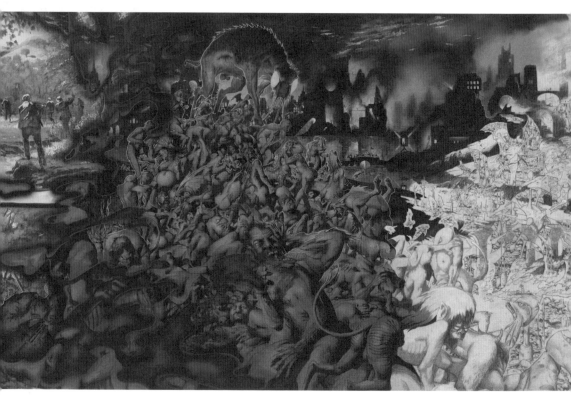

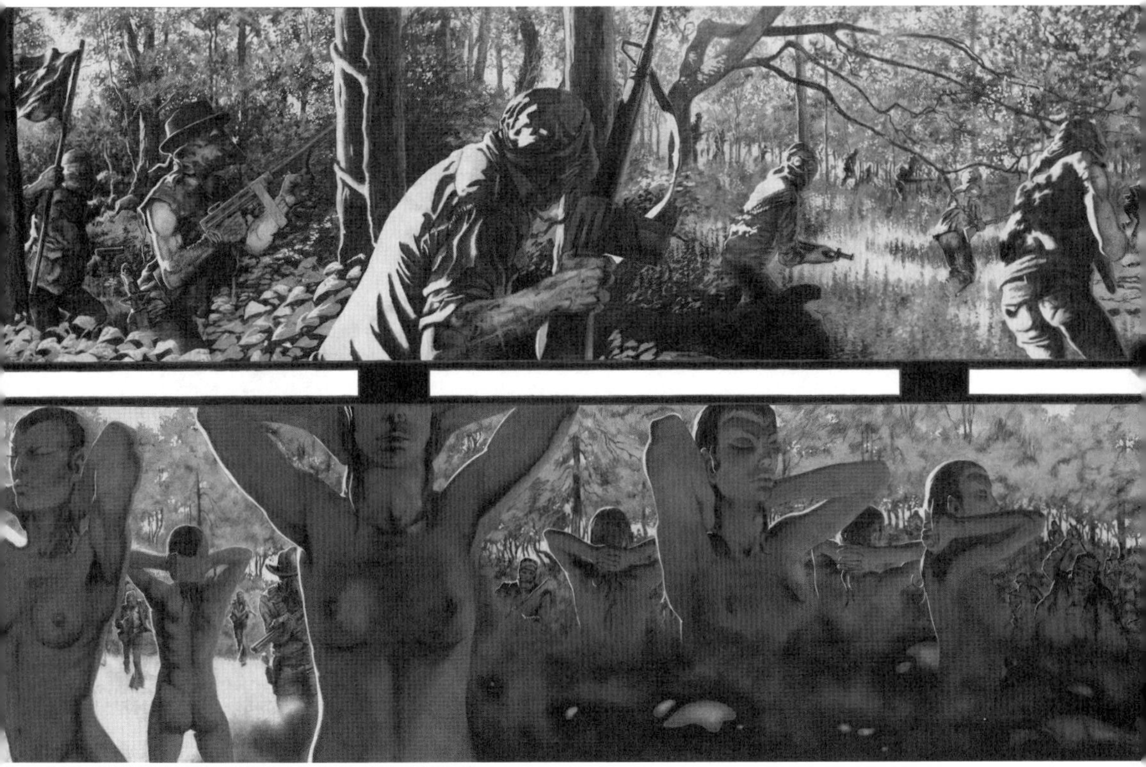

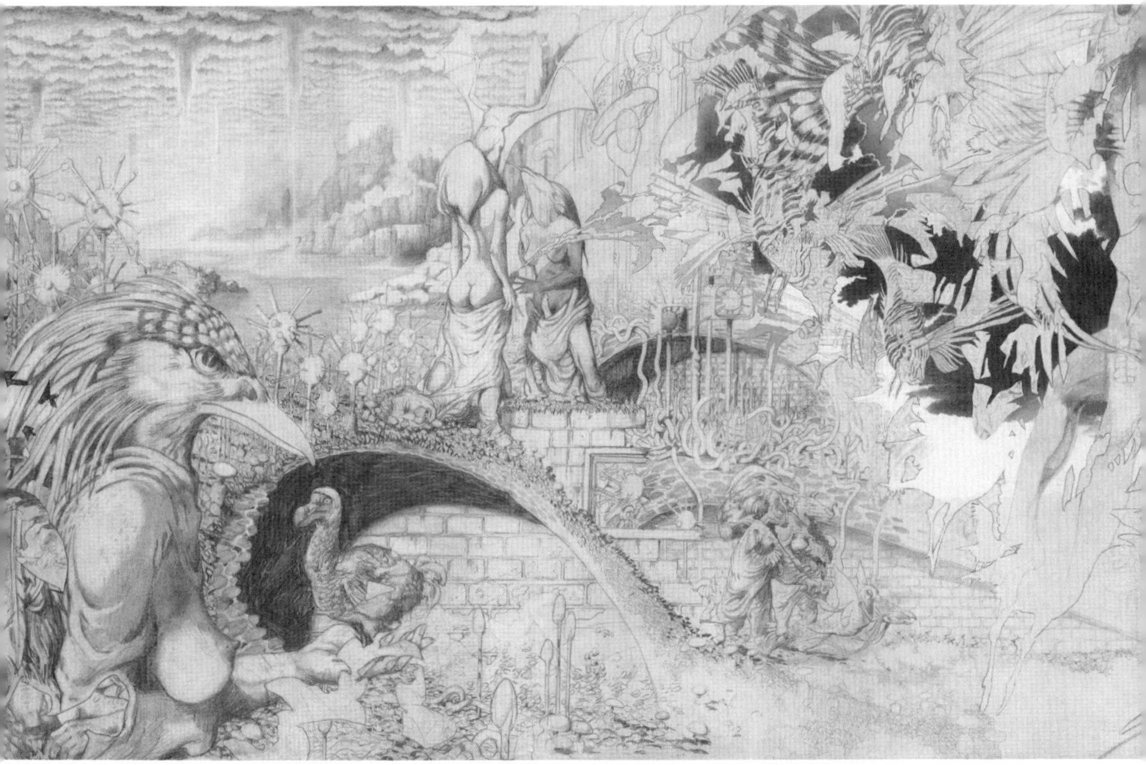

National Screw Magazine

Crawdaddy Magazine 2 of 6

National Screw Magazine

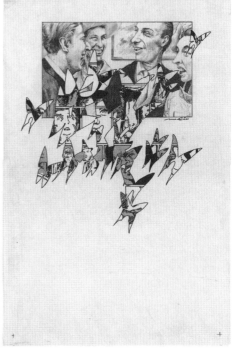

Exterminator! 2 of 4

Text only *Ah Pook* cover

Cumhu T-shirt

176

Mr. Hart 1970: "How did this happen?"

for owen
my God-son
william S. Burroughs
+ July 17, 1996

ENDNOTES

1   *"Ally Pally, as it was called..."* A fire at the Alexandra Palace in 1980 forced the Hornsey Fine Art Department — now part of the Middlesex Polytechnic — to relocate to a former chocolate factory, and from there — when it became part of Middlesex University — to a building known as the 'Cow Shed' in 2003. A progression somehow in keeping with Andy Warhol's effect on the art world over the same period of time.

2   *"...my enthusiasm for the entire project went downhill."* I began working on an alternative publication called *Finger*. The artists I'd met, including Jim Leon, Chris Achilleos, and Paul Sample also held off from contributing to *Cyclops*.

3   *"...The muddle of art theory and left wing agendas."* The Sit In raised questions about the methods of teaching and creating art, which was a legitimate wake-up call to a system that had gone uncontested for decades. It also attempted to clarify the role of the artist in society, in particular the academic standing of art students. The incorporation of the college into a polytechnic was contrary to that idea and an issue worth contesting. It was not achieved. Hornsey College of Art no longer exists as an autonomous entity.

4   *"...I'd taught myself taxidermy as a teenager."* I scoured the Dorset countryside on my bicycle looking for specimens — mostly road kills or corpses hung from vermin poles (a medieval-type device used by farmers for scaring away the living). In the event the remains weren't intact enough for stuffing, I brought a carving knife for removing parts worth saving. On one occasion I found a dead horse in a swamp and brought the head home. I became very sensitive to the smell of dead bodies as a result, not out of revulsion but simply because it meant that somewhere in the vicinity there was another subject for study. It was a good smell.

5   *"...reduced to less than a handful of battered, incomplete books."* "We found a large number of books in these characters and, as they contained nothing in which were not to be seen as superstition and lies of the devil, we burned them all, which they [the Maya] regretted to an amazing degree,

and which caused them much affliction." Bishop Diego de Landa, *Relacion De Las Cosas De Yucatan: 1566.*

6   *"Ah Pook !"* The original spelling was Ah Puch. Difficulty with the pronunciation led to the name being changed to Pook. Since this is now the official spelling, it has been used throughout this book. I regret the concession. There is much in a word, particularly a name — especially that of a god. It was the name that invoked the project.

7   *"...I just don't want to know about acid." Rolling Stone,* 1971. Interview with Robert Palmer.

8   *"...especially coming from inside a Morris Minor."* The Morris Minor was just over 12 feet long by 5 feet high — about the same size as a modern Mini/ BMW Hatchback. It was one of several car models used by the police in the 1960s and early 1970s nicknamed 'panda cars' for their black-and-white markings.

9   *"...English cops weren't as bad as American cops..."* Peter Watkins's film, *Punishment Park,* had just been released in London. It was a surreal anti-Vietnam-war movie about a camp in the Mojave Desert where law enforcement officers use convicted war protesters as training subjects. The young dissidents have to try to outrun and outwit their pursuers over a 60-mile trek though the desert. Inevitably, they're beaten and killed by the cops. It was a memorable film that was essentially banned in the United States. Major studios refused to distribute it, a clear indication of Hollywood's role with respect to the status quo. Burroughs knew Watkins.

10   *"...which amounted to at least 25 bombs..."* "The Angry Brigade," "1st of May Group," "Butch Cassidy and The Sundance Kid" and "The Wild Bunch" all made claims to bombings at the time.

11   *"The most brazen and disgusting attempt to corrupt..."* "Amok-Run of the Sexologists" from *Facing the Abyss,* A.K. Chesterton, 1976

12   *"...received hefty jail sentences* and *had their hair cut off."* In keeping with the times, 'hair' had been an issue during the proceedings. Whereas the judge and barristers *defined* authority with their farcical long hair wigs, the defendants were considered an affront to it by wearing their hair long naturally. Their jailers' response, like something out of Lewis Carroll, was to cut off the defendants' hair. All three were ultimately acquitted on appeal.

13   *"...an incongruous, Tardis-like structure in his bedroom, oddly reminiscent of an outhouse."* An Orgone Box was present in the loft on Franklin Street, in

the Bunker on the Bowery, and in Bill's home in Kansas — where Kurt Cobain also sat in. Whether or not it was the *same* Orgone Box and whether or not it traveled by conventional means is for others to determine.

14   *"The Old Man of the Mountain says..."* Hasan-i-Sabah was a historical figure popularized by Bill with respect to his role in training young male political assassins. The expression "do as thou wilt shall be the whole of the law," however, is generally ascribed to Aleister Crowley who, in turn, acknowledges Rabelais as the source. Referred to as the Law of Thelema, the line is from the novel *Gargantua: "Fay ce que vouldras."* Bill's combination of the two in the steakhouse was a mixture of artistic license and a goodly amount of scotch.

        In his book, *Templars and Assassins,* James Wasserman also suggests that even though Hasan-i-Sabah established the order of Ismaili *heyssessini* at the fortress of Alamut, he was not The Old Man of the Mountain of legend: "Hasan-i-Sabah's mission to the Ismailis of Syria resulted in the early European contact with the Assassins during the Crusades. The mythical Old Man of the Mountain, celebrated by troubadours and feared by kings, was the Syrian chief of the order."

15   *"... I wouldn't see or hear from either of them for 38 years."* Michel Choquette and his book would, in fact, resurface at exactly the same publisher at exactly the same time at as this book. *Someday Funnies* would finally be published by Abrams in 2011 and along with all the contributors (still alive) I was paid my 100 bucks.

16   *"...Reactive mind built in by our women who sent us"* — The unconscious, ancient parasite.

17   *"...'comic book' — something I'd wanted to avoid from the start."* Illustrators may have been below fine artists but comic artists were way below that. Associating the project in any way with comics reduced its credibility.

18   *"...seemed to completely belie the intensity of the fictional imagery he generated."* Bill once expressed his despair over people's reaction to his real-life persona. A guy in a jacket and tie seemed to be a disappointment to them, he said. "...they had expected me to appear stark naked with a strap-on, I presume." From "A Word to The Wise Guys" from *The Adding Machine,* ©1985 WSB.

19   *"Nobody seems to ask the question what words actually are...and what exactly their relationship is to the human nervous system."* from an interview with Gary Goldhill, BBC, 1963.

20 *"...the reason might have been the Angry Brigade."* As it happened, the so-called core members of the Angry Brigade had just been arrested and would be prosecuted that year in the longest English *criminal* trial on record. Angry Brigade activities still continued but the IRA also got in on the act around that time, using bigger bombs with far less concern for civilian casualties.

21 *"None of that art shit."* Private detective buddy Phil wore a suit, smoked reefer, and carried a hammer in his briefcase as he tried to figure out the perfect crime that would set him up for life.

22 *"Black Abductor, published in 1972..."* I was unaware of the book at the time.

23 *"No question about the star of the show."* In reference to the guy's cock. What's key in *Black Abductor* is that it's a 'black man's' cock — a prominent feature of 'white' sexual insecurity. As "Trish" herself describes it in the book: *"Human males simply did not have cocks that big. Donkeys, maybe, but not men. Her vision had to be playing tricks on her."*

24 *"I was stuck without a publisher, without a job, and with no money."* Journal and sketchbook entries during the first two years in the United States often describe being depressed about having no money and being unable to work. They were very difficult times emotionally as well as financially. Having the phone and electric constantly being disconnected and getting through days without money for food or even milk for tea are difficult to imagine but they are referred to enough times to confirm that the project often made me feel trapped. I mentioned my sense of despair over not being able to get it off my back several times. Self-portraits picture my head screwed to a drawing table.

25 *"Queimada."* A 1969 feature film directed by Gillo Pontecorvo starring Marlon Brando as Sir William Walker. A Vietnam War commentary that Brando considered one of his favorite films.

26 *...the Berkley Barb featured a four-page centerspread..."* From *A Conversation with Allen Ginsberg* by John Tytell,1974

27 *"No, man! It's not dope!"* Ted Morgan told me in 2007 that a couple of days after he gave Bill the 'aphrodisiac,' Bill called and said,*"Boy that stuff is great!"* Apparently I got out just in time.

28 *"...groups of 'art and literary' types."* Photographer Peter Hujar was among them and had just begun a series of group portraits titled "Friends." I sat in with Bill's group.

29 *"...he wouldn't 'shake hands with anybody from San Francisco.'"* From a

May 13, 1971 conversation among President Richard M. Nixon, John D. Ehrlichman, and H.R. Haldeman. Published in *Harpers Magazine*, Feb 2000 by James Warren.

30 *"He snapped like a dog..."* From "The Passing of Anatole Broyard" in *Thirteen Ways of Looking at a Black Man*. Henry Louis Gates, Jr., 1997

31 *"...savoring the rich folk lure of spells and curses."* Ah Puch is Here, early draft. (Spelling is inherent to words.)

32 *"So long as the calendar of animated cartoons..."* Ah Puch is Here, early draft.

33 *"...method for communicating ideas but* effective *nevertheless."* Inside the wardrobe I'd also discovered a folder titled *"Exterminator notes"* — also in Bill's handwriting. A collection of 60 or so pages of random ideas, including photocopies and originals. In amongst the stories and fragments was a page in which the origins of John Stanley Hart were finally confirmed:

> *"...Death rains back a hail of crystal skulls*
> *DEATH DEATH DEATH*
> *Go out and get the pictures. All the pictures of*
> *DEATH DEATH DEATH*
> *For Mr. Cane who didn't like to hear the word spoken in his presence*
> *DEATH DEATH DEATH*
> ...What is black and white and DEAD all over citizen Cane? Old newspapers in the wind frayed sounds of a distant city"

34 *"...I might achieve an alignment. A coincidence. Why not?"* Characters interacting with their creator were also the basis for Flann O'Brien's *At Swim Two Birds* — an author Bill had turned me on to and whose *Third Policeman* is still my favorite book. One of the characters in *At Swim Two Birds* was, coincidentally, a *"...Pooka... a species of human Irish devil endowed with magical powers."*

35 *"...the protagonist was a woman."* A naked one in fact, although this was not a pin-up type character. The point was to see the effect of a completely naked person when sex was not part of their motivation. It was ultimately self-defeating in terms of promoting the strip in other comics publications since kids read comics and the last thing *Gallery* needed was to be accused of encouraging them to look at naked women. As a result, Tetra went largely unnoticed by the 'comics' world.

36 *"...he became the adopted figurehead for the New York 'downtown' music scene."* In all the time I had known Bill I had never encountered him listening to music. Despite his many references to classic songs from his younger

days, he didn't mention any contemporary ones and I never once heard a radio or record player while I was around. On one occasion back in England, he had asked if I'd like to go to a Stones concert with him — he had backstage passes. I said no thanks. He agreed. "Last thing I want is to be stuck in amongst a bunch of screaming g-i-i-irls." My sentiments entirely — girls screaming at someone else, that is. I tried to introduce him to Frank Zappa's music and offered to lend him a couple of Zappa's albums. He seemed genuinely interested in the idea. A few months later, I asked him if he'd had a chance to listen to them. He was quite incredulous. "Well of course not, man! I don't have a record player!"

37 *"The end of a 'short, unhappy life,' at age 33." Cursed from Birth: The Short, Unhappy Life of William S. Burroughs, Jr.* — by William S. Burroughs Jr., edited and compiled by David Ohle. Soft Skull Press, 2006.

38 *"...an 'identikit' image of the producer..."* "I had an Identikit picture of Marty with me that Jim drew. It looks like a photo." *Cities of the Red Night*, p. 116. Bill had described my own image of Mr. Hart as an "identikit image," i.e., an image drawn from eyewitness accounts in order to recognize and apprehend a *character*.

39 *"...the methodology was the same as the one I'd used for Ah Pook."* "Jim sketches a scene in the rough. We stage it with live actors and then photograph it. Then Jim projects the color shots onto our paper for the finished product, which is something between photography and drawing..." *Cities of the Red Night*, p. 178.

40 *"Burroughs was being filmed..." Burroughs*, directed by Howard Brookner, 1983

41 *"The manner in which he compared himself to Billy..."* "See, I always felt funny dealing with Billy. I loved Billy, and — uh — felt like a brother to him. But you know how it is between brothers. There's a little rivalry. Especially if one brother is a ****-up and the other is an extraordinarily, competent, accomplishing person — which is the one that I was, of course."

"... I felt like he [Billy Jr.] looked at me as a reproach, a living reproach that I was the son that William wanted and not he." *James Grauerholz, Burroughs, 1983.*

42 *"...win me an Emmy."* Understanding the capabilities of the equipment and being able to choreograph imagery to suit often resulted in clients allowing free rein with the ideas also. The *Saturday Night Live* open was

one of them. I came up with the overall concept and the individual sight gags as well as the design for the piece. The storyboard was animated for timing and positioning of the actors, and the live action was superimposed over it on the studio monitor as it was shot.

43 *"Struck a blow to the whole diseased concept..."* From "A Word to The Wise Guys" from *The Adding Machine,* WSB 1985

44 *"...being buried in a Christian graveyard..."* Nor did Tibetan or Egyptian methods hold out much hope for him. His spoofs on the Egyptian routine were among his funniest bits. In Ah Pook, speaking through his alter ego Hart on the other hand, he wasn't keen on the idea at all: "Dead forever," he groaned. "Oh God think of it — me in deep freeze and nobody to thaw me out."

45 *"...have his ashes dropped into the straits from Cape Spartel."* From interview tapes for *Literary Outlaw: The Life and Times of William S. Burroughs* by Ted Morgan, 1982

46 *"...looking out over a bed of red roses..."* The photograph is by Burrough's art dealer, José Férez. The caption is in Burroughs's handwriting but it is interesting that he would refer to himself as "embalmed in roses" given his horror of the process and the fact that he was still alive.

47 *"Izzy the Push..."* "Certain pragmatic observations are useful for travellers in the magical universe. One law, or rather expectation, is that lightning usually strikes more than once in the same place." "On Coincidence," *The Adding Machine: Selected Essays,* WSB, 1986.

48 *"...more than a century-and-a-half ago."* Views of Ancient Monuments in Central America, Chiapas and Yucatan, published May 1844.

49 *"Cut the word lines the future leaks out"* From *The Job: Interviews with William Burroughs.* Daniel Odier, 1969. Published by Grove Press.

50 *"in which survivors eat the cabin boy ..."* From *The Narrative of Arthur Gordon Pym of Nantucket.* Edgar Allan Poe, 1838.

51 *"A ship considered unsinkable."* From *Futility, or the Wreck of the Titan.* Morgan Robertson, 1898. According to author Charles Pellegrino (*Ghosts of the Titanic*), a copy of the book was in the Titanic's library when it sank.

Prior to the Titanic sinking, the *SS Arctic* had been the frame of reference for civilian loss of life at sea. It's possible the *Arctic* inspired the *Titan* from the past rather than the *Titanic* from the future. It's likely that *Black Abductor* may have similarly 'inspired' the kidnapping of Patty Hearst and that the Fox *Lone Gunmen* episode did the same for the attacks on the World Trade Center Twin Towers.

52 *"... an attack on the buildings by a radio-controlled civilian airliner."* Fox's *The Lone Gunmen.* Broadcast March 4, 2000.

53 *"...more and more security."* A visit to Catherwood's birthplace in London during the course of writing this book was a real-life version of the totalitarian world I'd designed for the *Yes* video 20 years before: CCTV cameras perched on phone poles, trees, and building ledges were as ubiquitous as pigeons.

54 *"A uniformity of environment that precludes evolutionary mutations."* The *Western Lands,* WSB, p. 192.

55 *"...Suddenly 2012 has come to represent the possible mother of all 'Nighs.'"* One can only wonder whether the 1 in 8 preppers/survivalists who are on them have considered the consequences when the "normalizing" psychotropic drugs run out.

56 *"...a modern day Noah's Ark movie."* The SS *"I'm All Right, Jack"* (and sister ships) each the size of a small city built in complete secrecy by Chinese workers without tickets.

57 *"Everything is determined by that which it is not."* Color theory 101: Red exists by virtue of not being green and vice versa. Without both there is no color at all.

58 *"Maya* scholars..." including Simon Martin, author of *Chronicle of The Maya Kings and Queens,* with whom I corresponded.

59 *"Astronomy* scholars..." including Dr. Shephard Simpson.

60 *"...both a barometer of time* felt *and an odometer measuring time* spent." To the Ancient Egyptians, the heart was also the measure of life. It was weighed against a feather at the moment of death to determine the integrity of the individual.

61 *"As Don Frey Bartolomé de Las Casas and the good Bishop Landa himself pointed out."* A *Brief Report on the Destruction of the Indians.* Bartolemé de Las Casas, 1552. *Relacion De Las Cosas De Yucatan.* Diego de Landa Calderon, c. 1566.

62 *"...appalling horror and misery for young and old alike."* "I, Diego de Landa, say that I saw a great tree near the village upon the branches of which a captain had hung many women, with their infant children hung from their feet." *Yucatan Before and After the Conquest* by Friar Diego de Landa, 1566.

63 *"Even the pyramid."* Conspiracy nuts not withstanding, why *is* there

a pyramid alongside the Judeo/Christian God word on 21st century American money? Stone buildings of this nature were never a feature of North American history.

64 *"...numerological significance."* Western *and* Eastern numerological systems agree on the interpretation the number 11. *Tai*, the eleventh hexagram of the I-Ching — "heaven below, earth above" represents harmony and balance. 11 also figured prominently in the history of Ah Pook. The Dresden Codex is 11 feet long. The unspeakable Mr. Hart existed originally as 11 pages. 11 pages were ultimately published in *Rush* magazine. I intended to stay in America for only six months but would not return to England for 11 years. The implications of 9/11 would begin the process of reviving *Ah Pook* and it was announced in 2011 for publication the following year.

65 *"... he was able to face them down."* At the critical moment, the governor of Jerusalem — an acquaintance of Catherwood's, arrived in the Mosque with his entourage. He assured the angry crowd that the Englishman bore the firman of the Pasha Mohammed Ali himself and was required to survey the building in order to affect its repair. They should leave him to go about his business or they would answer to him personally. Catherwood was known for his "seven shot revolver," an idea that might have appealed to Bill Burroughs.

66 *"...Saladin restored it to the tenure of the Moslems once more."* After the Six-Day War in 1967, Israel commandeered the building.

67 *"The artist is drawn to it in order to draw from it."* This was demonstrated for me by the unlikeliest of people, in the unlikeliest of places, the first time I quit *Ah Pook*. When I was picking up my unemployment check at the Labour Exchange in London, the scruffy guy ahead of me moved to the side instead of leaving with his money. As the woman cashier was handing me mine, he placed a small cake on the counter in front of me.

"Do you know what gravity is?" he asked.

"Well yeah..." I said.

"No you don't," he said. "Here, see this cake? There's gravity between you and it, there's gravity between her and it, and there's gravity between me and it. But the gravity between me and it is a whole lot stronger. You know why?"

"Why?"

"Because I'm fucking starving."

68 *"... now push this pencil."* From an interview with Jurgen Ploog, *"The Commissioner of Sewers"* Documentary, 1986. 'Pencil pusher' is a job description not applicable to artists and nowadays rarely involves the use of an actual pencil.

69 *"If you can't do that, then where is it? It doesn't exist."* Interview with Jurgen Ploog, 1986.

70 *"...To be THE"* From *Electronic Revolution* in *The Job* by Daniel Odier. U.S. publisher 1970 Grove Press.

71 *"...an aberration of some kind."* Getting *back* to Nature: a linear Biblical/ Darwinian perspective.

72 *"They can switch in a heartbeat."* Every generation has its flat earth theory. Cigarette smoking is one of ours. In the course of twenty years, the *fact* that smoking is healthy — a *fact* endorsed by doctors — became *fiction*. It was replaced by the *fact* that it was the opposite. Implicit in that exchange is the idea that the fact was *inherently* fiction. Or both fact *and* fiction at the same time. It may conceivably switch priorities again.

73 *"...to seduce readers into a particular form of attentiveness."* 'Hoax' is an inevitable outcome of this factual/fictional dynamic. When Frederick Catherwood arrived in New York City, one the greatest proponents of the idea — P.T. Barnum — was at that moment in the process of conceding his very first. The 161-year old slave Josie Heth, whom Barnum had claimed had been owned by George Washington's father, had died and an autopsy had determined her to be merely half that age. As Barnum would insist however, presenting fiction as fact in a "glittering performance" was the means "by which to suddenly arrest the public's eye and ear." To seduce the audience into the consideration of the possibility.

74 *"...quite rightly the "Croaker..."* "*Croaker*: A doctor. *Write*: To write a narcotic prescription." *Junky*, WSB 1953

75 *"A month ago I'd turned 23."* The image of the Fly God cutting his wrists is from reference photos taken of me, aged 23.

76 *"...a man whose career was determined by "accident."* "In examining Stephens's career, one must believe in the providence of accidents. Stephens became a world-traveler by accident; he became a writer by accident, and these two accidents produced the explorer, with the result that such a bevy of accidents led to one purpose — now no longer accidental: to the discovery of the Mayan civilization." *The Search for the Maya; The Story of Stephens and Catherwood* by Victor von Hagen.

77 *"...a man dogged by a 'poltergeist'."* She was referring to Von Hagen's account of the fire on Prince Street that destroyed much of Catherwood's work. "The fates had been unkind to Catherwood. His great work on the Dome of the Rock at the Mosque of Omar was left unpublished; his pioneer work among the Egyptian tombs swallowed up in the anonymity of the unpublished folios of Robert May [sic], still lying in the British Museum collections, and now his great work on the Maya was destroyed." Von Hagen, *ibid*. In his book, *"Frederick Catherwood Archt."*, von Hagens also used the term specifically, adding, "What was this spiteful demiurge that always seemed to be in attendance on Frederick Catherwood?"

78 *"...no portrait or even written description of him is known to exist."* An illustration by Catherwood of a man surveying a Mayan temple is considered to be a self-portrait by some. It's a very small, full-figure drawing that can hardly be described as a recognizable likeness.

79 *"...his name alone was absent from both the survivors' and the victims' lists."* In *"Frederick Catherwood, Archt.,"* Victor von Hagens wrote: "Not a word of the friend of Keats, Severn, Shelley; and, in America, of Prescott, Bancroft, and Stephens; not a word of the companion of Bonomi, Robert Hay, and Wilkinson; the pioneer of Egyptology, the architect-draftsman of the Mosque of Omar, the panoramist of Leicester Square, the New York architect, the co-discoverer of the Mayan culture, the builder of South America's first railroad, the Argonaut of California. The New York newspapers, which over a period of fifteen years had printed many news releases on one of the greatest archaeological-explorers who ever lived did not once mention his name. That is until many days had passed... Then as a sort of afterthought, Catherwood appeared in a single line under 'The Saved and the Lost' — Frederick Catherwood Also is Missing".

80 *"...the number of lifeboats was not the issue."* Bill writes about lifeboats on a couple of occasions: Dr. Benway makes his debut appearance in one, seating himself amongst the ladies as the *SS America* goes down. And in *The Adding Machine*, it's a metaphor used to explain the drawbacks and limitations of Control. Two armed crewmembers take control of a lifeboat and force the other occupants to do the rowing. They control the food and water and only ration it sufficient to keep the others alive. It's a balancing act where the right degree of threat and minimum reward must constantly be maintained.

81 *"He just wants it to end."* In his final hours, Catherwood faced the most

terrifying of panoramas: a line of encirclement broken only by the rising and falling of the force that would consume him. This remark together with the opening reference to a man being "in a fog" can obviously be construed as standard medium parlance. In this case, however, they have particular relevance when placed within the context of a man who actually drowned in a fog and who was mentally very much 'with me' at the time. Given the typical questions that subjects present in these circumstances, regarding lost relatives, loved ones, etc., and the need to define matters concerning money, career, health, and romance, the fact that a man who was not 'related,' described as occupying an area of spirit far back in time, would be revealed within the first few minutes is noteworthy. That 'he' would then describe himself in such a manner, is a coincidence which again questions mathematical probability.

82 *Women and Children Last* by Alexander Crosby Brown. ©1961 Alexander Crosby Brown. Published by Van Rees Press, New York.

83 *"Once this reciprocating process is acknowledged it's difficult to disavow it."* Catherwood died when the *Arctic* sank. His partner, John Stephens, died the day the ship named in Stephens's honor was launched. The *SS Arctic* left Liverpool on her final voyage on September 20, 1854. The *SS John Lloyd Stephens* was launched from New York on September 21, 1852.

84 *"In his second book on Titanic..."* Charles Pellegrino, *Ghosts of the Titanic: New Discoveries from the Ocean Floor.* ©2000 Charles Pellegrino. Morrow.

85 "Fallen *into place, that is...*" Falling invariably suggests downward motion. Time and space in reality, however, do not have direction. Like the astronaut in *2001*, falling in these terms amounts to tumbling un-*controll*ably in no direction at all.

ACKNOWLEDGEMENTS

Art isn't *what* you make, it's what it makes of *you* — it's where it takes you. As a book, *Ah Pook is Here* was a disaster. As a journey of discovery, it was remarkably successful. The images are the map of that journey.

In the process of unfolding, it took me to places that were unprecedented and introduced me to people I could not have imagined. The more unusual among them prompted this book. *"I am a mapmaker charting unexplored areas of the psyche,"* said Bill. I acknowledge and thank them for adding a few more coordinates in that endeavor.

It was also a literal journey, both physical and emotional. I left the country where I was born on account of it, to learn another language, another geography, another cultural point of view. I would be made to change my many English preconceptions about America and, by making America my home, then do the same in reverse. The images would open doors and give me access to individuals who would privilege me with their own creative perspectives. It would give me firsthand insights into the worlds of book production, newspapers, magazines, television, film, and galleries. Above all, it would lead me to friends who would endure — most significantly the one to whom this book is dedicated.

To recount all the people who contributed to a project spanning decades is next to impossible, for many reasons, not the least of which is that regardless of diaries and sketchbooks, and lasting friendships, there are some people whose names I've simply forgotten.

Many of these people have hopefully been thanked by inclusion in the text. Even where their role may appear contrary, nevertheless they were essential to the effect and I thank them also.

People who helped me with *Ah Pook is Here* in England, who aren't named specifically in the text are Jennifer Seaton, Bob Mazzer, Katharine Atherley, Tom McLaughlin, Richard Sloggett, Edwin Belchamber, Alan Byrne, Lionel Stott, Andy Wardle, Felon Black, Mike Tebb, Paul Saunders, Marshall Fisher, Ernie Eban, Andrew Tweedy (and his girlfriend), and my brothers Alistair, Kevin, and Graham. In San Francisco, Brian Carter,

Peter Taylor, Dava Kuhlman, Lois Stopple, and Nancy Shatskin. In New York, Sharron Hedges, Ann Patty, David Dalton, Barbara Mallorek, Barbara Gitler, and Stephen Lemberg.

Observed While Falling was considered by several publishers but Gary Groth at Fantagraphics was the one who determined that it *should* be published. He negotiated with sincerity and determination for almost a year to make this book and the original collaboration possible. My agent, Joe Spieler, backed him throughout that process and I am indebted to them both. They have been invaluable allies. Mike Catron at Fantagraphics edited this book and *The Lost Art of Ah Pook is Here*. Tony Ong designed them. A fortunate coincidence indeed. Along with Jason Miles and the rest of the folks at Fantagraphics, they confirmed I was in the right place.

For the chance remark that initiated *Observed While Falling*, I thank Doug Apatow, and for introducing us, Barbara Munch. For pointing out the often very big gaps between the words, Sara Van Ness, Jim Pennington, Jamie Fettis, Steve Hull, Laura Williams, Cote Zellers, David Zung, Earl Mc Grath and Max Blagg, (Max pointed me to several Burroughs references particularly the "black dog" and mention of curses in Ted Morgan's biography.) I thank Sara also for her caring and insightful overview of the project in *The Lost Art of Ah Pook is Here*, the image version of the project.

For reading, promoting and generally encouraging: Ted Morgan, Colin Wilson, Michael Moorcock, George Laughead, Keith Seward, Oliver Harris, Jan Herman, Larry Sawyer, Eric Fournier, Michael Rothenberg, Tony O'Neil, Jed Birmingham, Spencer Tandy, Mariarosa Sclauzero, Rebecca Bailen, David Anthony, Vicky Bugbee, Rodrigo Salomon, Tej Hazarika, Michael Butterworth, Richard Adams, and Neal Beck.

In keeping with the mutual spirit of the internet, Jamie Fettis, an expert on 'albatrosses' appeared out of 'nowhere' to put an end to book burning and remind me of just who I was dealing with. Jamie, who was then completing his film of Coleridge's *Ancient Mariner*, not only provided relentless encouragement for the project, but assisted me with research and did whatever he could to impress the artwork and text onto gallery owners, writers, publishers, producers, lawyers, and even psychics. For keeping the project afloat, year after year, while dismissing any form of financial consideration, he has my unqualified respect and gratitude.

Finally, I would thank Frederick Catherwood — and his writer partner, John Stephens. Catherwood inspired the imagery in *Ah Pook is Here* and the recollection of its process in this book. It's the acknowledgement that any artist owes to another who has 'preceded' him, particularly one who has had such a far-reaching effect. The lines and brush strokes in someone else's art reveal a decision-making process that is timeless. They're the tangible evidence of a life lived within similar constraints. In Catherwood's case, that much more so. They're markers within a far larger picture: the infinite map of the mind. They point to the greater possibilities of travel — those which can be felt but not explained. Those which cannot be Controlled.